LIVERPOOL TO RUNCORN

including branches to Garston, Widnes and Warrington

Adrian Hartless

MP Middleton Press

Front cover: On 10th February 2007 LMS 8P 4-6-2 no. 6201 Princess Elizabeth *runs through West Allerton with Past Time Rail's* 'The Merseyside Express', *London Euston – Liverpool Lime Street and return. The Princess Royal Pacifics were regular power for Liverpool – London expresses between 1932-62 so this was an authentic re-enactment, and for a bonus the fireman, smiling for the camera, is the photographer's son. (D Birmingham)*

Back cover: Railway Clearing House map, dated 1947. The route of the album is shown with a dotted line.

Abbreviations:
Albright & Wilson (AW)
British Oxygen Co (BOC)
Cheshire Lines Committee (CLC)
Freightliner Terminal (FLT)
Garston Car Terminal (GCT)
Great Western Railway (GWR)
Imperial Chemical Industries (ICI)
Integrated Rail Plan (IRP)
Liverpool & Manchester Railway (L&M)
London & North Western Railway (LNW)
London, Midland & Scottish Railway (LMS)
Northern Powerhouse Rail (NPR)
Overhead Line Electrification (OLE)
Power Signal Box (PSB)
Railway Operating Centre (ROC)
St Helens & Runcorn Gap Railway (SHRG)
St Helens Canal & Railway Co (SHCR)
Traction Maintenance Depot (TMD)
TransPennine Express (TPE)

ACKNOWLEDGEMENTS

This book is dedicated to the memory of Vic Mitchell, ever enthusiastic and supportive, who encouraged his contributors 'to have fun, fun, fun!', and also to Michael (Mick) Young (1941-2020), another great railway enthusiast with whom I visited locosheds far and wide in the dying days of steam and who signalled many a London/Liverpool express through Polesworth and Tamworth. Grateful thanks are due to the 8D Association and especially Doug Birmingham, Paul Wright and Mike Turner without whom this book would have been greatly diminished, and to Judith Wilde at Catalyst Museum, Widnes. And true to the spirit of this series a special thank you to Jill for her patience during the long hours of compiling. Thanks also go to Godfrey Croughton, Geoff Gartside, Chris Howard, Norman Langridge, David and Dr Susan Salter and Michael Stewart.

Published June 2022

ISBN 978 1 910356 72 2

Cover design Deborah Esher
Production Cassandra Morgan

Published by
Middleton Press Ltd
Camelsdale Road
Haslemere
Surrey
GU27 3RJ
Tel: 01730 813169
Email: info@middletonpress.co.uk
www.middletonpress.co.uk

Printed and bound by CPI Group (UK) Ltd, Croydon, CR0 4YY

SECTIONS

CONTENTS

This volume breaks with the usual Middleton Press practice of presenting journeys in the down direction of travel, in order to better present the routes as radiating from Liverpool Lime Street.

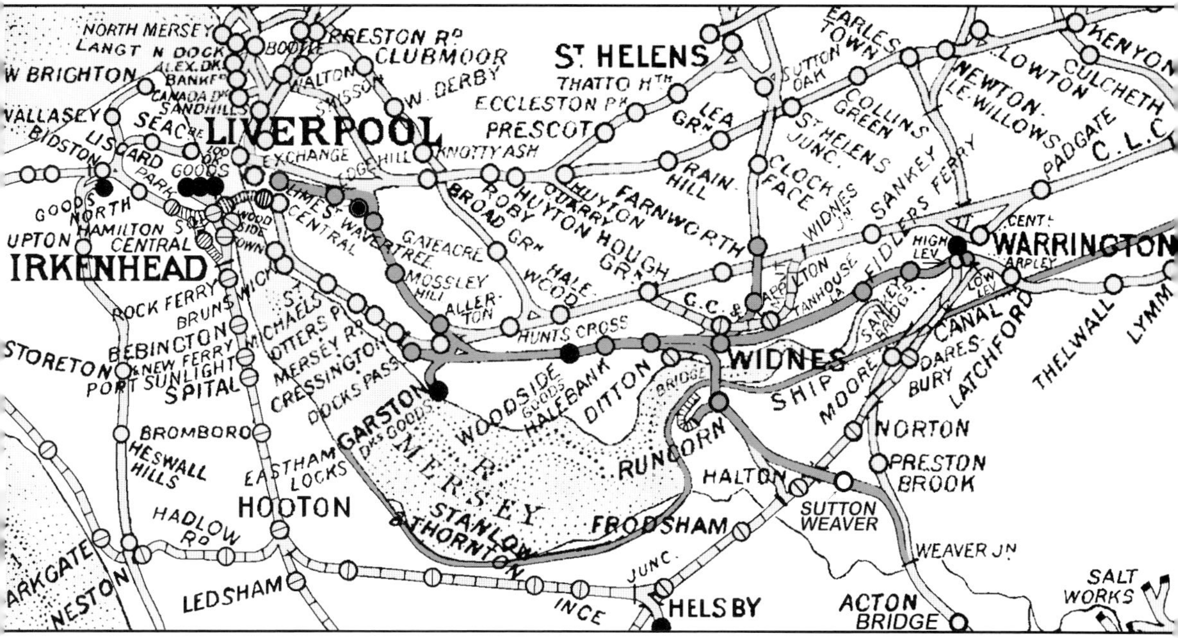

I. The Railway Clearing House map of 1947 has the route of this album in dark grey. Other maps in this album are derived from 25ins to 1 mile maps, with north at the top unless otherwise indicated.

GEOGRAPHICAL SETTING

The area covered by this volume is largely defined by the Mersey Estuary. This starts at Warrington Bridge and gradually widens as it flows westward until it encounters Runcorn Gap, a brief narrow stretch where the towns of Runcorn and Widnes developed on the south and north banks respectively. By the time it reaches Ellesmere Port and Speke the river is three miles wide, but then it gradually funnels to around 1,250 yards between Birkenhead and Liverpool, beyond which it flows into Liverpool Bay.

Historically the river was the boundary between Cheshire and Lancashire, but the local government reorganisation of 1974 made sweeping changes. The City of Liverpool, which extends eastward beyond Halewood, became part of Merseyside, a new ceremonial county. Runcorn and Widnes were combined administratively into the new Borough of Halton, which is part of the ceremonial County of Cheshire. At the same time Warrington was ceremonially moved from Lancashire to Cheshire.

There are not many hills in this district. Liverpool is partly built on a ridge of sandstone that parallels the Mersey and faces all eastward routes from the riverside. Runcorn occupies a hill that rises to almost 250ft and which precedes the watershed between the Mersey and its tributary the River Weaver at the southern end of our journey.

II. **Gradient Profile**

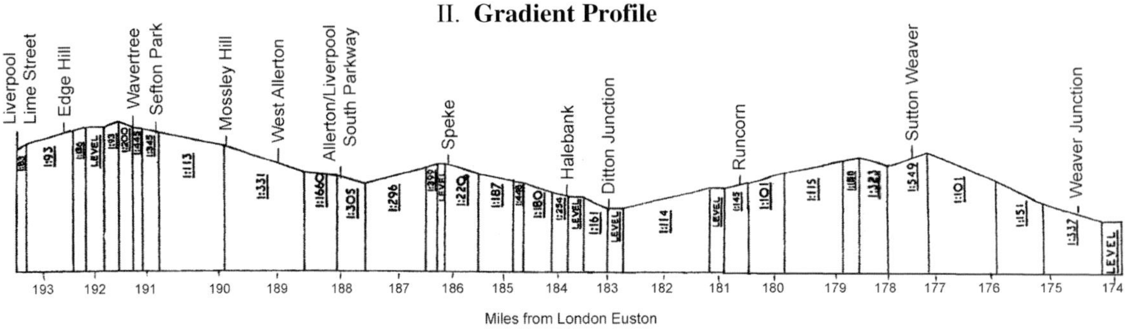

HISTORICAL BACKGROUND

The first railway in the district was the famous Liverpool & Manchester (L&M) which opened on 15th September 1830; our route utilises it for around 30 chains east of Edge Hill. Next to open was the St Helens & Runcorn Gap (SHRG) Railway on 21st February 1833. This was primarily a coal haulage business, connecting collieries in the St Helens area with a purpose-built dock at Runcorn Gap (Widnes).

The L&M quickly found its Liverpool terminus at Crown Street was poorly located and on 15th August 1836 it opened 1½ miles of new railway to larger and more central premises at Lime Street, which remains to this day Liverpool's principal railway station. For the next 33 years services to London and Manchester alike ran along the L&M as far as Earlestown before going their separate ways. Meanwhile the L&M had been taken over by the Grand Junction Railway which itself became a constituent of the London & North Western (LNW) Railway from 1st January 1846.

The SHRG merged with the Sankey Canal Co, its main competitor, in 1845, and began a period of growth as the St Helens Canal & Railway Co (SHCR). On 1st July 1852 it opened a seven-mile line along the north bank of the Mersey from Runcorn Gap to Garston where a new dock was built, larger than at Widnes and closer to the open sea. On 1st February 1853 it opened eastward from Runcorn Gap to Warrington where it linked with the Warrington & Stockport Railway.

From 1st September 1860 the LNW leased the SHCR, taking it over entirely from 31st July 1864. On 15th February 1864 the Edge Hill-Speke Junction line was opened, linking the L&M with the Garston line. This was the first tangible step in the LNW's plan to shorten the London – Liverpool route that was fully realised from 1st April 1869 when the Weaver Junction – Ditton Junction line opened to passengers. This involved the construction of Runcorn Bridge to cross the Mersey Estuary.

Final steps in the area's Victorian rail development were the opening on 1st November 1869 of the Widnes Deviation, an east–west bypass of the Widnes Dock area, which had become impossibly congested, and on 1st January 1873 of the Garston Curve, permitting direct travel between Lime Street and Garston Dock.

This network remained intact until 1947 when the Garston Dock passenger service was withdrawn. The first loss under British Railways was the St Helens – Ditton Junction passenger service, successor to the SHRG, from 18th June 1951. The Manchester – Warrington – Ditton Junction passenger service last ran on 8th September 1962. The SHRG line continued with freight until closure from 1st November 1981. Ditton – Warrington saw a significant increase in traffic when the coal fired Fiddlers Ferry Power Station was commissioned in the late 1960s. However, this closed on 31st March 2020 leaving the route with few residual trains.

On the positive side Crewe – Liverpool via Runcorn was one of BR's earliest main line electrification schemes with regular passenger services starting from 1st January 1962. On 30th October 1977 Merseyrail opened the City Loop beneath central Liverpool including an underground platform at Lime Street providing frequent services to the Wirral. In 2005-06 Allerton, for many years an unremarkable outer suburban station, was transformed into Liverpool South Parkway, a transport hub with low level platforms on Merseyrail and a frequent bus link to Liverpool John Lennon Airport. In 2017-18 the platforms and track at Lime Street were reconfigured in the station's biggest refurbishment since the 1870s.

PASSENGER SERVICES

1.1. Liverpool to London

This was one of the earliest inter-city journeys in the world, established in 1838. The original route was via Newton Junction (later Earlestown) – Warrington – Crewe – Birmingham Curzon Street where it was necessary to change from the Grand Junction to the London & Birmingham until 1846. Bradshaw for January 1845 showed seven down trains of which the quickest was the 10.00am ex-Euston, scheduled 8¼ hours to Lime Street. Improvements followed as steam locomotives grew stronger and track and signalling were made more robust. There were significant route improvements also; in 1847 the Trent Valley line opened between Stafford and Rugby, by-passing Birmingham and saving 7¾ miles, and in 1869 the Runcorn cut-off saved a further 8¼ miles. Cable haulage between Lime Street and Edge Hill ended the following year, avoiding the stop at Edge Hill to attach a locomotive. By the late 1890s there were four up expresses timed at 4¼ hours and two more taking a further 10 minutes. There was also a night sleeper, a service that lasted until late in the 20th century. By 1938, the year in which steam trains ran faster than ever before or since, there were two expresses timed from Liverpool in 3hrs 20 mins (the 10.10am 'Merseyside Express' and the 5.25pm). The outbreak of World War II and its aftermath ruled out further improvements with steam power.

The completion of 25kV AC overhead line electrification (OLE) to London in early 1966 revolutionised the service with expresses routinely allowed 2¾ hours whilst the twice daily Liverpool Pullman took 10 minutes less with stops at Runcorn and Watford Junction. This was for a while the fastest scheduled train on BR requiring an average speed of 82.3mph on the 163 mile down run between the intermediate stops. However, the Pullman was not a commercial success and was discontinued in May 1975. The arrival of the Pendolino tilting trains in 2001 reduced the schedule to 2 hrs 12 mins generally including stops at Runcorn, Crewe and Stafford. In April 2022 there were 17 departures Monday-Friday operated by Avanti West Coast.

1.2. Liverpool to Birmingham

This service is as old as the Grand Junction Railway, dating from 1837. It was soon subsumed by the London route and after the opening of the Trent Valley line was usually achieved by a change of train at Crewe or Stafford. The 1938 timetable showed five through up services. The BR Inter-City era brought more direct trains, mostly continuing to destinations such as Reading, Poole, or Bristol. These ended with privatisation and it fell to London Midland to service the route. In April 2022 this comprised an hourly service taking 1¾ hours with up to 10 stops including Liverpool South Parkway and Runcorn.

LIVERPOOL, RUNCORN, HARTFORD, and CREWE.—L. & N. W.

Mls	Fares. 1 cl.	2 cl.	gov	Return. 1 cl.	2 cl.	gov	Lime Street Sta.,	mrn	mrn	mrn	mrn (Breakfast Cars.)	mrn	mrn (Luncheon Cars.)	mrn	mrn	mrn (Bristol Express.)	mrn	mrn (Drawing Room Car Express.)	non	aft	aft (Saturdays only.)	aft
—							Liverpool ....dep.	2 35	....	7 20	8 0	8 15	9 45	9 50	10 5	1030	....	11 5	12 0	1210	1 40	2 0
—	0 4	0 3	0 1½	0 6	0 4	0 3	Edge Hill	....	....	7 25	8 5	8 20	9 50	9 55	1010	1035	....	1110	12 6	1215	1 45	2 6
—	0 4	0 3	0 2	0 7	0 5	0 4	Wavertree	....	....	....	....	....	....	10 0	....		....	....	....	....	....	....
—	0 5	0 3	0 2½	0 8	0 6	0 4	Sefton Park	....	....	....	....	....	....	10 2	....		....	....	....	....	....	....
—	0 6	0 4	0 3	0 8	0 7	0 6	Mossley Hill *	....	....	7 30	d	8 24	a	10 5	....		....	a	....	....	....	a
—	0 8	0 6	0 5	1 0	0 9	0 8	Allerton †	....	....	....		8 27		10 9	....		....	a	....	....	1 51	....
—	0 8	0 6	0 5	1 0	0 9	0 8	Speke	....	....	....		....		1013	....		....		....	....	....	....
—	1 6	0 10	0 8½	2 8	1 7	1 5	Halebank	....	....	....		....		1019	....		....		....	....	....	....
—	1 8	1 0	0 10½	2 11	2 0	1 9	Ditton Junc. 389	....	....	....		....		1025	....		....		....	....	....	....
—	2 9	1 5	1 3	4 6	2 9	2 6	Runcorn	....	7 30	....		8 40		1030	....		....		1224	1233	2 12	....
—	3 3	1 9	1 7	5 4	3 4	3 0	Sutton Weaver	....	7 36	....		....		1041	....		....		....	....	2 18	....
—	4 4	2 4	2 1	7 3	4 7	4 2	Acton Bridge 311, 400 arr.	....	7 45	7 54		....		1050	....	11 3	....		....	....	2 26	....
							Acton Bridge dep.	....	....	7 55		....		....	....	11 7	1110		....	....	....	....
—	4 10	2 7	2 4	8 0	5 2	4 8	Hartford 388	....	....	d		8 59		....	....	....	1117		....	....	....	....
—	5 9	3 1	2 9	9 6	6 1	5 6	Winsford	....	....	....		9 10		....	....	....	1127		....	....	....	....
—	6 9	3 6	3 2	10 6	6 5	5 10	Minshull Vernon	....	....	....		....		....	....	....	1135		....	....	....	....
—	7 0	3 11	3 6	12 0	7 9	7 0	Crewe 318, 338, 406 ar	3h20	....	8 20		9 22		....	1055	1125	1145	12 0	1255	1 5		2 56
—	12 3	8 2	7 4½	24 6	16 3	14 9	Derby 406 ....arr.	9 43	....	1032	....			....	1 10	....	....	....	....	3 20		....
—	13 0	9 6	7 6	26 0	16 6	15 0	318 Birmingham .. "	6e10	....	1050	1050	....	....	....	1220	....	....	2 30	2 50	....		....
—	29 0	20 8	16 6	58 0	36 2	33 0	319 London (Euston) "	7b10	....	1215	1215	2 0	2 0	....	....	....	....	3 30	5 15	....		6 25

For other Trains, see page 388. Continued below.

Lime Street Sta.,	aft	aft	aft	aft (Bristol Express.)	aft (Dining Cars.)	aft	aft	aft	aft	aft (Dining Cars.)	aft	aft	aft (Via Warrington.)	aft (Sleeping Saloon Exp.)		SUNDAYS. mrn	mrn (Via Warrington.)	mrn	aft (Dining Cars.)	aft	aft (Sleeping Saloon Express.)	
Liverpool ....dep.	2 20	2 40	....	3 25	4 5	4 10	4 35	5 10	5 30	6 15	6 50	7 0	1045	1155	....	2 35	9 20	1130	4 5	4 30	11 0	....
Edge Hill	2 25	2 45	....	3 30	4 10	4 15	4 40	5 15	5 35	6 20	6 55	7 5	1050	12 0	....	....	9 25	1135	4 10	4 35	11 5	....
Wavertree	....	....	....	....		....	....	....	....		....	7 10			....	....		....		....		....
Sefton Park	....	....	....	....		....	....	....	....		....	....			....	....		....		....		....
Mossley Hill *	....	....	....	i		....	....	....	5 42		....	....			....	....		....		....		....
Allerton †	2 34	....	....			....	....	a	5 46		....	7 16			....	....		....		....		....
Speke	....	....	....			....	....	....	5 51		....	7 20			....	....		....		....		....
Halebank	....	....	....			....	....	....	....		....	7 26			....	....		....		....		....
Ditton Junc. 389	2 41	....	....			....	....	....	5 59		....	7 29			....	....		....		....		....
Runcorn	2 47	....	....			4 34	....	5 33	6 5	6 39	....	7 36		1220	....	....		....		....		....
Sutton Weaver	2 55	....	....			4 42	....	....	6 14	....	....	7 44			....	....		....		....		....
Acton Bridge 313, 400 arr.	3 5	....	....			4 51	....	....	6 22	....	....	7 54			....	....	1040	....		....		....
Acton Bridge dep.	3 6	....	....			4 53	....	....	....	....	....	7 55			....	....	1041	....		....		....
Hartford 388	3 11	....	3 49			5 j 2	....	5 52	....	6 57	....	8 2			....	....	1049	....		....		....
Winsford	....	....	3 57			5 24	....	....	....	....	....	8 10			....	....	1059	....		....		....
Minshull Vernon	....	....	f			5 30	....	....	....	....	....	8 16			....	....	....	....		....		....
Crewe 320, 339, 406 ar	....	3 33	4 11	4 20	4 57	5 40	5 28	6 10	....	7 15	7 42	8 25	12 6	1250	....	3 20	1113	1230	4 57	5 25	1155	....
Derby 406 ....arr.	....	6 5	....	....	....	....	....	8 56	....	....	....	....	....	....	....	1120	....	....	....	8 0	....	....
320 Birmingham .. "	....	5 0	....	....	....	7 35	6 55	8 25	....	....	9 20	11½k	....	2 32	....	6 10	....	2 50	....	7 30	2 32	....
321 London (Euston) "	....	....	....	8 c0	8 20	9 25	9 25	1025	....	10¾c	....	....	3c50	6 0	....	7 10	....	4 35	8 20	....	3g50	c

For other Trains, see page 388.

a Stop to take up for South of Stafford on notice being given at the Station. b Arrives at 8 mrn. on Mondays. c 1&3 class. d Stop to take up for London on notice being given at the Station. e Arrives at 5 45 mrn. on Mondays. f Stops to set down on informing the Guard. g Sleeping Saloon arrives at 4 16 mrn. h Arrives at 3 55 mrn. on Mondays. i Stops to take up for Shrewsbury and beyond on notice being given at the Station. j Departs at 5 15 aft. k Arrives at 10 15 aft. on Mondays and Saturdays. * Station for Aigburth; † for Garston and Woolton.

☞ For other Trains between Liverpool and Ditton Junction, see pages 388 and 390; between Acton Bridge and Crewe, see pages 318 to 324.

↑ Bradshaw, July 1899 ↓ LMSR, 1938

LIVERPOOL, RUNCORN, ACTON BRIDGE, HARTFORD and CREWE

Week Days.

Miles	Up.	mrn (Except Mondays.)	mn		mn (To Northwich, p. 530)	mn (One class only.)	mrn D		mrn	mrn (RC Exp. to London.)		mrn (Breakfast served; West of England RC Exp.)		mrn Z	mrn RC (The Merseyside Express. RC Southport to London, page 565.)		mrn (To Northwich, see page 530.)		mrn	mrn (RC Exp. to London.)		W noon		aft	aft S		aft (Liverpool to London Exp.; Teas & a la carte meals served on Train. RC Southport to London page 565.)		aft E
	Liverpool (Lime Street) dep.	2 30	615	..	..		8 0	..	8 5	8 15	..	9 10	..	9 40	1010	..	10 10	..	..	1115	..	12 0	..	12 5	1 5	..	2 15	..	2 20
1¾	Edge Hill		620	..	..		..	..	8 10	..	..	9 15	..	9H45	..	..	10 15	..	..	..	..	12 5	..	12 10	1 10	..	..	..	2 25
2¼	Wavertree		623	..	..		..	..	8 13	..	..		..	..	..	..	10 20	..	..	..	..	..	..	12 13	..	..	..	..	..
3	Sefton Park		625	..	..		..	..	8 15	..	..		..	..	..	..	10 22	..	..	..	..	..	..	12 15	..	..	..	..	..
3¾	Mossley Hill, for Aigburth		628	..	..		8 8	..	8 18	8H23	..		..	9H50	Bb	..	10 25	..	..	H1123	..	..	..	12 18	..	..	2H23	..	2 33
5¾	Allerton C		[illegible]	..	..		..	..	8 22		..		..	..		..	10 29	..	..		..	..	..	12 22	..	..		..	2 37
9⅝	Halebank		..	..	..		..	..	8 29		..		..	..		..	10 36	..	..		..	..	..	12 29	..	..		..	..
10⅝	Ditton Junction 540, 601		[illegible]	..	743		..	..	8T40		..		..	..		..	10/53	..	..		..	..	..	12 40	..	..		..	2 46
13½	Runcorn		..	..	748		8 23	..	8 45		..	9 33	..	..		..	10 58	..	..		..	12 24	..	12 46	1 28	..		..	2 53
21½	Acton Bridge 436, 530 arr.		..	..	8 3		..	..	8 59		..	..	..	..		..	11 12	..	..		..	..	..	12 59	1 41	..		..	3 8
	Acton Bridge dep.		..	..		8 8	..	..	9 0		..	..	..	..		..		..	1120		..	..	..	1 0	1 42	..		..	3 15
23¾	Hartford B		..	..		814	8 38	..	9 5		..	9.49	..	..		..		..	1125		..	..	..	1 5	1 47	..		..	3 20
28¼	Winsford A		..	..		..	..	..	9 12		..	..	..	..		..		..	1132		..	..	..	1 12	1 55	..		..	3 30
30¾	Minshull Vernon		..	..		..	..	..	9 17		..	..	..	..		..		..	1137		..	..	..	1 17	..	..		..	3A49
35⅝	Crewe 424, 488, 530 arr.	3 20	..	..		..	8 55	..	9 26	9 [illegible]	..	10 6	..	1036		..		..	1147	12 3	..	12 55	..	1 33	2 18	..	3 5	..	4 5
68½	488 Shrewsbury (Gen.) arr.	7 12	..	..		..	..	..	..	1022	..	1120	..	..		..		..	..	1 25	..	1 56	..	3S9	..	..	4 41	..	5 56
188¾	488 Bristol (T.M.) "	..	..	..		..	..	..	..	..	..	2 30	..	..		..		..	..	..	..	5 20	..	..	..	..	..	..	..
88⅝	425 Birmingham (New St) "	7 0	..	..		..	..	..	..	1039	..	..	..	12 2		..		..	..	1 57	..	2*54	..	..	..	..	5 0	..	..
193¾	425 London (Euston) "	6 35	..	..		..	..	..	..	12 0	..	1R10	..	R 2d48	1 30	..		..	..	3 5	..	5 33	..	5XR50	5R50	..	6 5	..	..

Week Days—Continued. / **Sundays.**

Up.	aft (Birmingham and West of England Express.)	aft (RC Exp. Liverpool to London.)	(Exp., Liverpool to Birmingham)	aft E		aft (To Northwich, page 530.)	aft a (RC Liverpool to Birmingham except Sats.)	(RC Express to London.)		aft E	aft S	aft	(Birmingham & West of England Exp.)	aft		aft E	aft S	aft Y (London & West of England Express.)		Sundays mrn (RC Exp. to London.)	mrn r (Express, Liverpool to London.)	mrn (Express to Birmingham.)	mrn RC (W. of England Exp.)		aft Z (Liverpool to London.)	aft Z (RC Exp. to London.)	aft (RC Exp. to London.)	aft (Exp. to Birmingham & Coventry, p. 475. RC to Cardiff, p. 489.)	aft	aft SC (Exp., Liverpool to London.)
Liverpool (Lime Street) dep.	3 0	4 10		4 20	..	5 10	5 25		..	5 30	5 30	7 5		7 20	..	10 0	10 0	1150	..	9 30	10 0	1020	10 40	..	1 0	4 25	5 50	7 22	1045	1155
Edge Hill				4 25	..	5 15			..	5 35	5 35	7 10		7 25	..	10 9	10 9	1155	..			..	10 45	..	1 5	4 30		..	1050	12 0
Wavertree				..	..	5 18			..	..	..	..		7 30	..	..	..	..	..			..		..		..		..	..	..
Sefton Park				..	..	5 21			..	..	..	..		7 32	..	..	..	..	..			..		..		..		..	..	..
Mossley Hill, for Aigburth				..	..	5 24			..	..	..	..		7 35	..	..	..	..	..			..		..		..		7 31	..	..
Allerton C				..	..	5 27			..	5 42	5 42	..		7 39	..	..	..	..	..			1031		..		..		7 36	..	..
Halebank				..	..	5 34			..	..	..	..		7 46	..	..	..	..	..			..		..		..		..	..	..
Ditton Junction 540, 601				..	..	5d43			..	..	..	..		7 50	..	..	..	..	..			..		..		..		..	..	..
Runcorn	3 20			415	..	5 49			..	5 55	5 55	7 28		7 57	..	1028	1028	1218	..	9 50		1044	11 4	..		..		7 48	11 9	1218
Acton Bridge 436, 530 arr.				455	..	6 2			..	6 8	6 8	..		8 10	..	..	1041	..	..	..		..	..	..		..		..	..	
Acton Bridge dep.				456	..				..	6 10	6 16	..		8 11	..	..	1042	..	..	..		..	..	..		..		..	..	
Hartford B				5 [illegible]	..				..	6 15	6 22	..		8 16	..	1048	1048	..	..	..		..	11 22	..		5 5	6 22	..	1126	
Winsford A				510	..				..	6 22	6 29	..		8 21	..	1055	1055	..	..	..		..	..	..		..	..	..	..	
Minshull Vernon				..	..				..	6 28	6 34	..		8 3[illegible]	..	..	..	..	..	..		..	..	..		..	..	..	..	
Crewe 424, 488, 530 arr.	3 54	4 53		541	..		6 8		..	6 52	6 46	7 58		8 38	..	1110	1110	1253	..	1024	1049	1118	11 40	..	1 50	5 23	6 39	8 19	1143	
488 Shrewsbury (General) arr.	4 51	7S5		7 5	..		..		..	7 58	..	9 9		10*30	..	..	1233	2 8	..	..	1230	..	12 40	..	..	..	..	1040	2 8	
488 Bristol (T.M.) "	8 5	..		..	..		..		..	10F52	..	1230		..	..	..	..	5 35	..	..	..	..	4 4	..	..	..	..	..	5 35	
425 Birmingham (New St.) "	5 25	6 37		..	..		7x57		..	8 19	..	9 46		11 41	..	2 15	2 15	4K50	..	..	..	1252	2 2	..	3 52	7 20	..	8 57	2 15	6 16
425 London (Euston) "	..	7 40		..	..		8 45		..	10R40	1040	R		4 e1	..	5 0	4 50	5K35	..	1 45	2 10	..	4 5	..	5 40	9 10	9 35	..	4 50	5 27

A Sta. for Wharton (½ mile) and Over (2¼ miles). A Arr. 3 36 aft. a Thro Carr., Southport to London p. 565. B 1 mile to Hartford and Greenbank Sta. Bb Stops at 10 21 mrn. to take up for London. C Sta. for Garston and Woolton. D Thro Train to Nuneaton, p. 426. d Arr. 2 41 aft. on Sats. E or E Except Sats. F One class only (Limited accommodation) for portion of journey. H Stops to take up only. K Arr. Birmingham (N.S.) at 7 13 and London (E.) at 5 45 mrn. Suns. l Arr. 10 40 mrn. R Restaurant Car, Crewe to London. r 3rd class Restaurant Car to London. RC Restaurant Car. SC 1st & 3rd cl. Sleeping Accommodation. S or S Sats. only. T Arr. 8 33 mrn. TC Thro Carr. x Arr. 5 38 aft. e Except Sun. morns. Via Birmingham. W West of England RC Exp. TC to Birmingham, Aberystwyth (pp. 488 & 143) and Swansea, p. 492. X Arr. 5 10 aft. on Mons. and Sats. x Arr 8 19 aft. on Sats. Y 1st & 3rd cl. Sleeping accommodation and Thro Carrs., Liverpool to London. y Arr. 12 33 aft. Z Thro Carr. to Birmingham. Z Bournemouth and Southampton Exp. Thro Carrs., Liverpool to Bournemouth W. and Southampton (C. and Term.), pp. 426, 656, 78, and 188. Thro Carrs. to Birmingham. * 5 mins. later Sats.

1.3. Liverpool to the South West

The LNW and London, Midland & Scottish Railway (LMS) ran daily services to Bristol, usually including Great Western Railway (GWR) carriages, and mostly travelling via Crewe – Shrewsbury – Hereford. BR continued the pattern until the mid-1960s when the surviving services all ran via Birmingham, which was more remunerative. Following privatisation it has not been possible to catch a through train from Liverpool to Bristol.

1.4. Liverpool to Crewe

The local service via Runcorn dates from 1869. The July 1899 timetable showed five down services. Three called at all 14 intermediate stops; only one up service did this, although its schedule included a 20 minute layover at Acton Bridge. Electrification greatly improved the service frequency; in 1982 there were 15 departures Monday-Friday serving all (by now) 9 stops in the peaks and otherwise omitting Edge Hill and Ditton. Following privatisation the service was effectively withdrawn with Edge Hill – Allerton served instead by Northern and Runcorn – Winsford by London Midland.

LIVERPOOL, RUNCORN, FRODSHAM, HELSBY, and CHESTER.—London and North Western.

Fares. 1 cl.	2 cl.	gov	Lime-Street,	mrn	mrn	mrn	mrn	mrn	mrn	mrn	mrn	mrn	mrn	mrn	mrn	non	aft	aft	aft	aft	aft	aft	aft
			Liverpool ....dep.	6 25	....	....	7 15	7 30	8 20	8 40	....	9 5	9 50	1020	11 0	....	....	1240	1250	1 15	1 25	1 40	....
0 4	0 3	0 1½	**Edge Hill**	6 30	....	....	7 20	7 35	8 25	8 45	....	9 10	9 55	1025	11 5	....	....	1245	1255	1 20	1 30	1 45	....
0 4	0 3	0 2	Wavertree	6 35	....	....	Mondays only.	....	8 30	....	....	....	10 0	....	....	....	....	To Llandudno.	....	....	1 34	....	....
0 5	0 3	0 2½	Sefton Park ....[burth.	6 37	....	....		....	8 32	....	....	....	10 2	....	....	....	....		....	....	1 36	....	....
0 6	0 4	0 3	**Mossley Hill** (for Aig-	6 40	....	....		7 41	8 35	8 51	....	9 18	10 5	1033	....	....	....		....	1 26	1 39	....	....
0 8	0 6	0 5	Allerton (for Garston	6 45	....	....		7 45	8 39	8 55	....	9 22	10 9	1037	....	....	....		1 4	1 30	1 43	1 51	....
0 8	0 6	0 5	Speke...[and Woolton)	6 50	....	....		....	8 43	....	....	....	1013	....	....	....	....		....	Sats. only.	1 47	....	....
1 6	1 0	0 8½	Halebank	6 56	....	....		....	8 48	....	....	....	1019	....	....	....	....		....		1 53	....	....
1 8	1 0	0 10½	Ditton Junction	6 59	7 10	....		7 55	8 51	....	9 17	9 29	1025	....	....	12 0	....		....		1 56	....	2 22
2 9	1 5	1 3	**Runcorn**	....	7 16	....		8 1	9 1	9 7	9 25	....	1030	1054	....	12e8	....		1 20		....	2 4	2 27
2 10	1 11	1 6	Frodsham **356**	....	7 28	7 57		8 15	....	....	9 35	....	....	11 3	1131	1226	1250	....	....	1 58	....	f	2 36
2 10	1 11	1 6	Helsby **354**	....	7 33	8 2		8 25	....	....	9 40	....	....	....	....	1231	1256	....	....	2 8	....	Sat.	2 41
2 10	1 11	1 6	Dunham Hill	....	....	8 7		....	....	f	....	....	....	....	....	....	1 1	....	....	....	....	....	....
2 10	1 11	1 6	Mickle Trafford	....	....	8 13		....	....	....	....	....	....	....	....	....	1 6	....	....	....	....	....	....
2 10	1 8	1 6	**Chester 358, 357**.arr.	....	....	8 25	8 5	8 35	....	9 35	....	....	....	1120	1153	....	1 15	....	1 43	2 18	....	2 32	....

Week Days—*Continued.* / **Sndys**

Lime Street,	aft	aft	aft	aft	aft	aft	aft	aft	aft	aft	aft	aft	aft	aft	aft	aft	aft	aft	aft	aft	aft	Sndys mrn	Sndys aft
Liverpool ....dep.	....	3 30	4 0	4 0	4 20	....	4 50	5 10	....	5 20	5 30	6 5	6 25	7 15	....	8 30	9 45	10 5	1045	1110	1155	9 20	1045
Edge Hill	....	3 35	Except Saturdays. To Llandudno.	4 6	4 25	....	4 55	5 15	....	5 25	5 35	6 11	6 30	7 20	....	8 35	9 50	1010	1050	1115	12 0	9 25	1050
Wavertree	....	....		Saturdays only.	4 30	....	....	....	....	5 30	....	6 15	....	....	....	8 40	....	1015	Via Warrington.	1120	....	Via Warrington.	Via Warrington.
Sefton Park ....[burth	....	....			4 32	....	....	....	....	5 32	....	6 17	....	7 25	....	8 42	....	1017		1122	....		
Mossley Hill (for Aig-	....	....			4 35	....	....	....	....	5 35	5 42	6 20	....	7 29	....	8 45	9 56	1020		1126	....		
Allerton (for Garston	....	3 42			4 39	....	....	h	....	5 40	5 46	6 24	....	7 33	....	8 49	b	1024		1131	....		
Speke...[and Woolton)	....	....			4 43	....	....	....	....	....	5 51	6 28	....	....	....	8 53	....	....		....	....		
Halebank	....	....			4 49	....	....	....	....	5 47	....	6 34	....	....	....	8 58	....	1034		Sat.	....		
Ditton Junction	3 40	3 50			4 53	5 0	....	....	....	5 50	5 59	6 38	6 46	....	....	9k1	....	1038		1142	....		
Runcorn	3 45	3 57			....	5 5	5 15	5 35	5 40	....	6 5	....	6 50	7 48	....	9 15	1011	....		1147	1220		
Frodsham **356**	....	4 8			....	....	5 24	....	5 50	....	....	....	6 59	7 57	8 3	....	1022	....		1159	....		
Helsby **354**	....	4 13			....	....	5 30	....	5 55	....	....	....	7 4	8 1	8 8	....	c	....		12 4	....		
Dunham Hill	....	4 18			....	....	....	....	....	....	....	....	Sig.	....	8 13	....	....	....		....	....		
Mickle Trafford	....	4 23			....	....	....	....	....	....	....	....	7 12	....	8 17	....	....	....		....	....		
Chester 359, 357.arr.	....	4 32		4 44	....	....	5 45	....	....	....	....	....	7 20	8 15	8 26	....	1045	....	12 5	1223	....	1050	12 5

Fares. 1 cl	2 cl.	gov		mrn	mrn	mrn	mrn	mrn	mrn	mrn	mrn	mrn	mrn	mrn	mrn	mrn	mrn	mrn	mrn	mrn	mrn	aft	aft	aft
			Chester ......dep.	1 32	4 35	4 35	....	7 5	....	7 25	....	....	....	8 50	9g22	9 40	....	....	10 5	1050	1148	....	....	....
0 6	0 4	0 3	Mickle Trafford...	Except Mondays. Via Warrington.	Except Mondays. Via Warrington.	....	....	7 15	....	7 34	....	....	....	....	Except Saturdays. From Llandudno.	9 47	....	....	....	1057	....	....	....	....
0 10	0 7	0 5	Dunham Hill....			....	....	7 22	....	7 42	....	....	....	....		9 52	....	....	....	11 2	....	....	....	....
1 3	0 10	0 7½	Helsby **354**....			....	....	7 31	....	7 49	8 20	....	....	9 5		9 57	10 2	....	....	11 7	1159	....	1 10	....
1 8	1 1	0 10	Frodsham **356**....			....	....	7 35	....	7 55	8 25	....	....	9 9		10 1	10 7	....	....	1111	12 4	....	1 15	....
2 6	1 4	1 2	**Runcorn 386**....			5 0	....	8 i 0	8 19	....	8 39	9 6	9 10	9 15		....	1015	....	1026	....	1216	1230	1 25	1 35
2 10	1 8	1 6	Ditton J. **390, 389**			Mondays only.	8 0	8 5	8 27	....	8 44	....	9 15	9 26		....	1021	....	1032	....	d	1240	1 32	....
2 10	1 8	1 6	Halebank				8 4	....	8 31	....	8 54	....	....	....		....	....	1024	....	....	....	1244	....	....
2 10	1 8	1 6	Speke....				8 10	....	8 37	....	9 0	....	....	....		....	....	1029	....	....	....	1250	....	....
2 10	1 8	1 6	Allerton * **393**....				8 16	....	8 43	....	9 5	....	....	9 35		....	....	1033	1041	....	1228	1255	....	....
2 10	1 8	1 6	Mossley Hill †				8 20	....	8 48	....	9 10	....	....	....		....	....	1037	....	....	....	1 0	....	....
2 10	1 8	1 6	Sefton Park....				8 23	....	8 51	....	....	....	....	....		....	....	....	....	....	....	1 3	....	....
2 10	1 8	1 6	Wavertree ...[400				8 25	....	8 53	....	....	....	....	....		....	....	....	....	....	....	1 5	....	....
2 10	1 8	1 6	EdgeHill **403, 386,**	3 30	5 35	5 20	8 29	8 23	8 58	....	9 16	9 27	....	9 44	10 0	....	....	1043	1050	....	1240	1 10	....	1 55
2 10	1 8	1 6	**Liverpool 352** arr.	3 35	5 40	5 25	8 35	8 30	9 5	....	9 22	9 35	....	9 50	10 5	....	....	1048	1055	....	1245	1 15	....	2 0

Week Days—*Continued.* / **Sundays.**

	aft	aft	aft	aft	aft	aft	aft	aft	aft	aft	aft	aft	aft	aft	aft	aft	aft	aft	aft	aft	aft	Sundays mrn	Sundays mrn	Sundays aft
Chester ......dep.	Sats. only.	....	2 0	2 10	....	....	3 40	....	4 48	....	....	5 30	....	5 55	....	8 0	9 0	....	9 40	1042	11 5	2 32	4 35	8 0
Mickle Trafford ..		....	....	2 17	....	....	....	....	....	....	....	....	....	6 2	....	8 7	....	....	....	Mondays only.	....	Via Warrington.	Via Warrington.	Via Warrington.
Dunham Hill....		....	....	2 22	....	....	....	....	....	....	....	....	....	6 10	....	a	....	....	9 50		....			
Helsby **354**....		....	....	2 27	2 47	....	....	....	....	....	....	....	6 9	6 15	....	8 16	....	....	9 55		Sig.			
Frodsham **356**....		....	....	2 31	2 52	....	3 54	....	5 2	....	....	....	6 13	6 20	....	8 20	9 15	....	9 59		1121			
Runcorn 386....		....	....	....	3 2	3 46	4 2	4 40	5 11	....	5 41	5 50	6 23	6 29	....	8 30	Sats. only.	9 53	1010		1132			
Ditton J. **390, 389**	1 39	2 20	....	....	3j40	3 53	....	4 46	....	5 38	5 47	....	6 29	....	6 45	8 37		10 7	....		Sat.			
Halebank........	1 42	2 23	....	....	....	3 56	....	....	....	5 42	....	....	....	....	6 49	....		1011	....		....			
Speke	....	2 28	....	....	....	4 1	....	Stop	....	5 48	....	....	....	....	6 55	....		....	....		....			
Allerton * **393**....	1 50	2 32	....	....	3 49	4 6	4 14	aft	5 23	5 53	5 55	6 3	....	6 43	7 0	8 45	9 38	1021	1022		Sat.			
Mossley Hill †	1 54	....	....	....	....	4 10	4 18	5 21	....	5 58	5 59	....	....	....	7 5	....	9 42	1026	....		....			
Sefton Park....	....	....	....	....	....	4 13	....	5 24	....	6 2	....	....	....	....	7 9	....	9 45	1030	....		....			
Wavertree....[400	2 0	....	....	....	....	4 16	....	5 26	....	6 4	....	....	....	....	7 11	....	9 47	1032	....		....			
EdgeHill **403, 386,**	2 5	2 39	2 45	....	3 58	4 20	4 25	5 31	5 33	6 8	6 5	6 13	....	6 52	7 14	8 58	9 51	1035	1030	1120	1150	3 30	5 35	1110
Liverpool 352 arr.	2 10	2 45	2 50	....	4 5	4 25	4 32	5 35	5 38	6 15	6 10	6 20	....	6 58	7 20	9 5	9 58	1040	1035	1125	1155	3 35	5 40	1115

a Stops to take up for Runcorn and beyond on notice being given at the Station. **b** Stops to take up for Chester and beyond on notice being given at the Station. **c** Stops to set down from Runcorn and beyond on informing the Guard. **d** Stops to set down from beyond Chester on informing the Guard. **e** Departs at 12 15 aft. **f** Stop to set down on informing the Guard. **g** Departs at 9 28 mrn. on Mondays. **h** Stops to take up for South of Stafford on notice being given at the Station. **i** Arrives at 7 44 mrn. **j** Arrives at 3 7 aft. **k** Departs at 9 10 aft.

* Station for Garston and Woolton; † for Aigburth.

☞ For **other Trains** between Liverpool and Runcorn, see pages 386 and 387; between Liverpool and Ditton Junction see pages 390 and 391; between Frodsham and Chester, see page 356.

Bradshaw, July 1899

1.5. Liverpool to Chester

This route commenced with the opening of the Frodsham Branch in 1873 and included through trains to the North Wales coast particularly during holidays. In the 1890s there were around 10 departures Monday-Friday taking roughly one hour. The regular passenger service was withdrawn from 5th May 1975 after which the branch was used only by summer Saturday trains. In 1994 the southbound line on the branch was removed following which the service was reduced to a single train once a week in summer only between Chester and Runcorn. Not surprisingly the branch was proposed for closure, but there was sufficient opposition from local authorities to prevent this, and eventually funding was forthcoming to upgrade it as the Frodsham Single. An hourly service between Liverpool and Chester operated by Transport for Wales was launched from 19th May 2019, however the frequency was reduced because of the COVID pandemic. TfW has announced its intention to extend the service to Cardiff, via Shrewsbury and Hereford.

Merseyrail runs from Lime Street to Chester via Birkenhead every 15 minutes for much of the day.

1.6. Liverpool (LS) to Warrington Central

This route was added to the Lime Street – Allerton section in 1966 when the former Cheshire Lines Committee (CLC) services from Manchester Central and Warrington Central were diverted from Liverpool Central. This brought an hourly stopping service to Edge Hill, Mossley Hill, West Allerton and Allerton which later became half-hourly, replacing the Crewe locals. Following Allerton's transformation to Liverpool South Parkway all services via Warrington Central call there including East Midland Railway's hourly Liverpool – Norwich trains.

2. Liverpool to Garston Dock

Garston was initially served from Runcorn Gap but after the Garston Curve opened in 1873 the service came from Liverpool Lime Street. In 1899 there were 17 departures each taking 23 minutes for the 7½ mile journey including 6 stops. Tram competition hit hard soon afterwards. By 1947, when the service was withdrawn, the number of departures had dropped to 3 (4 on Saturdays).

LIVERPOOL and GARSTON.—London and North Western.

Fares. 1 cl.	2 cl.	3 cl.	Lime Street Station,	mrn	gov	mrn	mrn	mrn	aft	aft	aft		aft	aft	aft	aft	aft	gov	gov	aft	aft	aft
s. d.	s. d.	s. d.	**Liverpool** ....dep.	7 0	8 55	9 55	1050	1145	1215	1255	1 50	**Sats. only.**	2 15	2 50	3 50	4 55	5 45	6 20	6 55	7 50	9 10	1030
....	....	....	Edge Hill	7 4	8 59	9 59	1054	1149	1219	1259	1 54		2 19	2 54	3 55	4 59	5 49	6 25	6 59	7 54	9 14	1034
....	....	....	Wavertree	7 8	9 3	10 3	1058	1153	1223	1 3	1 58		2 23	2 58	3 58	5 3	5 53	6 28	7 3	7 58	9 18	1038
....	....	....	Sefton Park	7 10	9 5	10 5	11 0	1155	1225	1 5	2 0		2 25	3 0	4 0	5 5	5 55	6 30	7 5	8 0	9 20	1040
....	....	....	Mossley Hill, fr Aigbrth	7 14	9 9	10 9	11 4	1159	1229	1 9	2 4		2 29	3 4	4 4	5 8	5 59	6 34	7 9	8 4	9 24	1044
....	....	....	Allerton *	7 18	9 13	1013	11 8	12 3	1233	1 13	2 8		2 33	3 8	4 8	5 12	6 3	6 38	7 13	8 8	9 28	1048
....	....	....	**Garston** (Church Road)	7 21	9 16	1016	1111	12 6	1236	1 16	2 11		2 36	3 11	4 11	5 15	6 6	6 41	7 16	8 11	9 31	1051
....	....	....	" (Dock Sta.) arr.	7 23	9 18	1018	1113	12 8	1238	1 18	2 13		2 38	3 13	4 13	5 16	6 8	6 43	7 18	8 13	9 33	1053
Fares. 1 cl.	2 cl.	3 cl.	Dock Station,	mrn	gov	mrn	mrn	mrn	mrn	aft	aft	aft	aft	aft	aft	aft	aft	aft	aft	aft		
			Garston ....dep.	7 40	8 25	9 5	9 30	9 55	11 5	12 5	1 5	1 30	2 0	3 5	3 50	5 5	6 10	6 50	7 15	11 5	....	....
....	....	....	" (Church Road)	7 42	8 27	9 7	9 32	9 57	11 7	12 7	1 7	1 32	2 2	3 7	3 52	5 7	6 13	6 52	7 17	11 7	....	....
....	....	....	Allerton * **386**	7 45	8 30	9 10	9 35	10 0	1110	1210	1 10	1 35	2 5	3 10	3 55	5 10	6 18	6 55	7 20	1110	....	....
....	....	....	Mossley Hill, fr Aigbrth	7 49	8 34	9 14	9 39	10 4	1114	1214	1 14	1 39	2 9	3 14	3 59	5 14	6 22	6 59	7 24	1114	....	....
....	....	....	Sefton Park	7 52	8 37	9 17	9 42	10 7	1117	1217	1 17	1 42	2 12	3 17	4 2	5 17	6 26	7 2	7 27	1117	....	....
....	....	....	Wavertree	7 54	8 39	9 19	9 45	10 9	1119	1219	1 19	1 44	2 14	3 19	4 4	5 19	6 29	7 4	7 29	1119	....	....
....	....	....	Edge Hill **403, 386** ...	7 58	8 43	9 23	9 50	1013	1123	1223	1 23	1 48	2 18	3 23	4 8	5 23	6 33	7 8	7 33	1123	....	....
....	....	....	**Liverpool 352** .... arr.	8 3	8 48	9 28	9 55	1018	1128	1228	1 28	1 53	2 23	3 28	4 13	5 28	6 38	7 13	7 38	1128	....	....

* Station for Garston and Woolton.

Bradshaw, July 1899

3. Ditton Junction to Warrington

The SHCR provided the earliest trains between Warrington – Ditton – Garston, and the route hosted a short-lived Great Northern service from London King's Cross – Garston from which enterprising passengers could end their journey to Liverpool by river boat. After the LNW took over, the main service was Liverpool – Ditton – Warrington – Manchester London Road. There were 10 such departures in 1899, serving up to 26 intermediate stations, and various short workings. The frequency gradually diminished, and by the time the service was withdrawn in 1962 Ditton Junction had become the westerly terminus for around half the trips. The Ditton Junction – Warrington section had quite uneven coverage in 1961 with 7 up trains Monday-Friday (5 on Saturdays) and only 3 down (2).

LIVERPOOL, WIDNES, WARRINGTON, LYMM, STOCKPORT, and MANCHESTER.—L. & N. W.

Fares. 1 cl.	2 cl.	gov	Return. 1 cl.	2 cl.	gov	Lime Street Station,	mrn	mrn	mrn	mrn	mrn	mrn	mrn	mrn	mrn	mrn	aft	aft	aft	aft	aft	aft
						Liverpool ....dep.	....	6 25	....	....	....	8 20	9 5	....	9 50	....	....	....	1230	1 25	....	Through Train. Llandudno to Leeds.
0 4	0 3	0 1½	0 6	0 4	0 3	Edge Hill.	....	6 30	....	....	....	8 25	9 10	....	9 55	....	....	....	1235	1 30	....	
0 4	0 3	0 2	0 7	0 5	0 4	Wavertree	....	6 35	....	....	....	8 30	....	....	10 0	....	....	....	....	1 34	....	
0 5	0 3	0 2½	0 8	0 6	0 4	Sefton Park	....	6 37	....	....	....	8 32	....	....	10 2	....	....	....	....	1 36	....	
0 6	0 4	0 3	0 8	0 7	0 6	Mossley Hill, fr Aigbrth	....	6 40	....	....	....	8 35	9 18	....	10 5	....	....	....	1241	1 39	....	
0 8	0 6	0 5	1 0	0 9	0 8	**Allerton**, for Garston	....	6 45	....	....	....	8 39	9 22	....	10 9	....	....	....	1245	1 43	....	
0 8	0 6	0 5	1 0	0 9	0 8	Speke... [and Woolton	....	6 50	....	....	....	8 43	....	....	1013	....	....	....	....	1 47	....	
1 6	0 10	0 8½	2 8	1 7	1 5	Halebank	....	6 56	....	....	....	8 48	....	....	1019	....	....	....	1252	1 53	....	
1 8	1 0	0 10½	2 11	2 0	1 9	Ditton Junction ..arr.	....	6 59	....	....	....	8 51	9 29	....	1022	....	....	....	1255	1 56	....	
2 9	1 5	1 3	4 6	2 9	2 6	**Runcorn** ....dep.	....	....	....	....	....	8 39	9 19	....	1015	....	1026	....	1230	1 25	....	
....	....	....	....	....	....	Ditton Junction ......dep.	....	7 1	7 10	....	....	8 53	9 30	9 35	1030	....	12 5	....	1256	1 58	2 10	
2 0	1 2	1 0	3 6	2 3	2 0	**Widnes 389**	....	7 5	7 13	....	....	8 56	9 33	9 38	1033	....	12 8	1216	1259	2 2	2 14	
2 8	1 6	1 3½	4 6	2 9	2 6	Fiddler's Ferry & Penketh.	....	7 12	Stop	....	....	9 5	9 43	Stop	....	....	Stop	1224	Sat.	2 9	....	
2 10	1 7	1 4½	4 6	2 9	2 6	Sankey Bridges	....	7 16		....	....	9 9	....		....	....		1228	....	2 13	....	
2 10	1 8	1 6	4 6	2 9	2 6	**Warringtn** (B.Q.) **364, 318**	....	7 19	....	....	....	9 12	9 48	....	1045	....	....	1231	1 10	2 16	....	
....	....	....	....	....	....	CHESTER (Gen) **356** dep.	....	4h35	mrn	7 25	....	....	8 45	....	1012	....	....	1140	....	1 23	....	2 30
....	....	....	....	....	....	**Warrington** (Bank Q.) dep.	....	7 20	7 55	8 30	8 57	9 14	9 55	....	1046	....	....	1233	1 11	2 20	....	....
2 10	1 8	1 6	4 6	2 9	2 6	**Warrington** (Arpley)	6 20	7 22	8 0	8 35	9 0	9 16	9 58	....	1049	....	....	1236	1 14	2 23	....	3 5
3 6	1 10	1 8	5 0	3 1	2 9	Latchford	6 25	7 28	8 4	8 39	9 4	....	10 2	....	1054	....	....	1240	1 18	2 27	....	....
3 10	2 0	1 10	5 4	3 5	3 1	Thelwall	6 33	7 33	8 9	8 44	9 8	....	10 6	....	1058	....	aft	1244	1 23	2 31	....	....
4 1	2 2	1 11	5 9	3 8	3 4	**Lymm**	6 40	7 38	8 14	8 50	9 12	....	1010	....	11 3	....	1253	1248	1 28	2 35	....	3 15
4 4	2 4	2 1	6 2	4 0	3 7	Heatley and Warburton	6 47	7 43	8 19	8 55	9 16	....	1014	....	11 8	....	1256		1 33	2 39	....	....
4 7	2 6	2 2½	6 8	4 3	3 10	Dunham Massey	6 54	7 48	8 23	9 0	9 20	....	1018	....	1113	....	1 0	....	1 37	2 43	....	....
5 0	2 6	2 3	7 6	4 7	4 2	Broadheath (Altrinchm) ar	7 1	7 53	8 28	9 7	9 26	....	1025	....	1118	....	1 5	....	1 41	2 50	....	3 23
....	....	....	....	....	....	**Broadheath** ....dep.	....	8 15	8 55	....	....	....	....	....	1130	....		....	1 48	....	....	3 24
5 4	2 10	2 6½	8 2	5 1	4 7	Northenden	....	8 28	9 2	....	....	....	....	....	1143	....		....	1 56	....	....	....
5 6	3 0	2 8	8 6	5 4	4 10	**Cheadle**	....	8 32	9 12	....	....	....	....	....	1148	....		....	2 1	....	....	e
6 0	3 1	2 9½	9 2	5 6	5 0	**Stockport 394, 402** arr.	....	8 37	9 18	....	....	....	....	....	1154	....		....	2 6	....	....	3 42
8 0	4 11	4 5	15 2	9 1	8 3	BUXTON **402** ......arr.	....	1017	1017	....	....	....	....	....	1254	....		....	3 35	5b15	....	5 15
....	....	....	....	....	....	Broadheath ....dep.	7 1	7 54	8 29	9 8	9 27	....	1025	mrn	1119	....	Saturdays only.	....	1 42	2 50	....	....
5 0	2 8	2 4½	7 6	4 9	4 3	Timperley	7 7	....	....	....	....	....	1028	1033	1123	1148		....	....	2 55	....	....
5 0	2 8	2 4½	7 9	4 9	4 3	Brooklands	....	....	....	....	....	....	....	1036	....	1151		....	1 46	....	....	....
5 0	2 8	2 4½	7 9	4 9	4 3	Sale & Ashton-on-Mersy	7 12	....	....	....	....	....	....	1039	1128	1154		....	1 49	....	....	....
5 0	2 9	2 6	8 0	5 0	4 6	Stretford	7 17	....	....	....	....	....	....	1044	....	1159		....	1 53	....	....	....
5 3	2 9	2 6	8 0	5 0	4 6	Old Trafford	7 22	8 5	....	....	....	....	....	1048	....	12 3		....	....	....	....	....
....	....	....	....	....	....	Knot Mill & Deansgate	7 27	8 10	8 48	9 22	9 42	....	1042	1054	1140	12 9		....	2 0	3 9	....	....
5 6	2 9	2 6	8 0	5 0	4 6	**Oxford Road**	7 30	8 12	8 50	9 24	9 44	....	1043	1056	1142	1210		....	2 2	3 10	....	....
5 6	2 9	2 6	8 0	5 0	4 6	**Manchestr** (Lon. Rd.*)	7 35	8 16	8 55	9 30	9 47	....	1048	....	1145	....		....	2 5	3 15	....	....

Other Trains, pp. 386 & 388 (Liverpool to Ditton Junction). Local Trains, page 392 (Timperley to Manchester).

Up—*Continued.*

Lime Street Station,	Week Days—*Continued.* aft	aft	aft	aft	aft	aft	aft	aft	aft	aft	aft	aft	aft	aft	aft	Sundays. mrn	aft	aft	aft
Liverpool ....dep.	2 40	....	3 35	4 20	....	5 20	....	6 5	....	7 0	8 30	....	10 5	1045	1110	7 35	2 10	7 15	1045
Edge Hill	2 45	....	3 40	4 25	....	5 25	....	6 11	....	7 5	8 35	....	1010	1050	1115	7 40	2 15	7 20	1050
Wavertree	2 50	....	....	4 30	....	5 30	....	6 15	....	7 10	8 40	....	1015	....	1120	7 45	2 20	7 25	....
Sefton Park	2 52	....		4 32	....	5 32	....	6 17	....	....	8 42	....	1017	....	1122	....	....	....	....
Mossley Hill, fr Aigbrth	2 55	....	....	4 35	....	5 35	....	6 20	....	....	8 45	....	1020	....	1126	7 50	2 25	7 30	....
Allerton, for Garston	3 0	....	....	4 39	....	5 40	....	6 24	....	7 16	8 49	....	1024	....	1131	7 55	2 30	7 35	....
Speke... [and Woolton	3 5	....	....	4 43	....	....	....	6 28	....	7 20	8 53	....	....	....	....	8 0	2 35	7 40	....
Halebank	3 11	....	....	4 49	....	5 47	....	6 34	....	7 26	8 58	....	1034	....	1138	8 6	2 41	7 46	....
Ditton Junction ..arr.	3 14	....	....	4 53	....	5 50	....	6 38	....	7 29	9 1	....	1038	....	1142	8 9	2 44	7 49	....
Runcorn ....dep.	3 2	....	....	4 40	....	5 41	....	6 23	....	....	8 30	9 53	....	....	1132	....	....	....	....
Ditton Junction	3 16	3 35	....	4 55	5 30	5 51	....	6 41	6 54	7 35	9 3	10 5	1041	....	1143	8 10	2 46	7 50	....
Widnes 389	3 20	3 38	3 58	5 0	5 33	5 55	....	6 46	7 0	7 38	9 6	10 8	1046	11 6	1146	8 14	2 50	7 54	11 6
Fiddler's Ferry & Penketh.	3 27	....	....	5 7	Stop	6 2	....	6 54	....	Stop	9 14	....	....	....	Saturdays only.	8 22	2 57	8 2	....
Sankey Bridges	3 30	....	....	5 11		6 6	....	6 58	....		9 18	....	....	....		8 26	3 1	8 6	....
Warringtn (B.Q.) **364, 320**	3 34	....	4 7	5 14	....	6 9	....	7 1	....	....	9 21	....	....	1115		8 29	3 4	8 9	1115
CHESTER (Gen) **356** dep.	3 0	....	....	3 50	....	5 10	....	5 40	....	....	8 50	....	....	10g0		6 30	....	6 55	8 0
Warrington (Bank Q.) dep.	3 35	....	4 9	5 15	Except Saturdays.	6 10	....	7 5	....	aft	9 25	....	....	1140		8 46	3 5	8 10	1140
Warrington (Arpley)	3 38	....	4 11	5 18		6 13	....	7 8	....	7 45	9 27	....	....	....		8 50	3 8	8 12	....
Latchford	3 42	....	4 16	5 22		6 18	....	7 12	....	7 50	9 32	....	....	....		8 55	3 12	8 18	....
Thelwall	3 46	....	4 20	5 26		6 23	....	7 16	....	7 55	9 36	....	....	....		9 0	3 16	8 23	....
Lymm	3 50	....	4 24	5 30		6 28	....	7 20	....	8 0	9 40	....	....	1150		9 5	3 20	8 28	a
Heatley and Warburton	3 54	....	4 28	5 34		6 33	....	7 24	....		9 44	....	....	....		9 9	3 24	8 33	....
Dunham Massey	3 58	....	....	5 38		6 38	....	7 28	....		9 48	....	....	....		9 13	3 28	8 38	....
Broadheath (Altrinchm) ar	4 4	....	4 34	5 43		6 44	....	7 34	....		9 53	....	....	....		9 19	3 34	8 44	....
Broadheath ....dep.	....	....	4 34	5 44		6 55	....	7 40	....		....	....	....	....		....	....	....	....
Northenden	....	....	....	5 55		7 3	....	7 48	....		....	....	....	....		....	....	....	....
Cheadle	....	....	4 44	6 2		7 8	....	7 53	....		....	....	....	....		....	....	....	....
Stockport 395, 402 arr.	....	....	4 50	6 7		7 13	....	7 58	....		....	....	....	1215		....	....	....	1215
BUXTON **402** ......arr.	....	....	5c45	7 20	aft	....	....	9 50	....		12 4b	d	....		....	....	7b23	....	
Broadheath ....dep.	4 5	....	4 40	....	6 25	6 45	....	7 35	....	Saturdays only.	9 54	....	....	Via Stockport.	....	9 20	3 35	8 45	Via Stockport.
Timperley	4 10	....	4 48	....	....	6 48	7 3	7 38	....		9 57	....	....		....	9 24	3 39	8 49	
Brooklands	....	....	....	....	....		7 6	....	....		10 0	....	....		....	9 27	3 42	8 52	
Sale & Ashton-on-Mersy	4 16	....	4 54	....	6 33	6 52	7 9	7 42	....		10 4	....	....		....	9 30	3 45	8 55	
Stretford	4 20	....	4 58	....	....	....	7 14	....	....		10 8	....	....		....	9 35	3 50	9 0	
Old Trafford	4 25	....	5 3	....	6 40	....	7 18	....	....		1012	....	....		....	9 39	3 54	9 4	
Knot Mill & Deansgate	4 31	....	5 9	....	6 46	7 0	7 24	7 56	....		1017	....	....		....	9 45	4 0	9 10	
Oxford Road	4 32	....	5 10	....	6 47	7 2	7 25	7 58	....		1019	....	....		....	9 46	4 1	9 12	
Manchestr (Lon. Rd.*)	4 38	....	5 16	....	6 50	7 5	....	8 2	....		1023	....	....	1230	....	9 50	4 5	9 15	1230

Other Trains, pp. 386 & 388 (Liverpool to Ditton Junction). Local Trains, page 392 (Timperley to Manchester).

a Stops to set down on informing the Guard. b *Via* Manchester.
c Arrives at 6 12 aft. on Saturdays. d Arrives on Thursdays and Saturdays.
e Stops to set down from Chester and beyond on informing the Guard.
Saturdays only. h Leaves at 2 20 mrn. on Mondays.
* South Junction Platform.
☞ For **other Trains** between Runcorn and Widnes, see page 389.

Bradshaw, July 1899

4. St. Helens to Runcorn Gap

In its early days the SHRG was a steam-worked waggonway that tacked a couple of carriages hired from the L&M onto its coal trains. There was no timetable and the only advertised stops were the two termini. Because the route initially included two rope-worked inclined planes it was said the 7¼ mile journey could be walked as quickly. The route was realigned to avoid the inclines and the railway had separated passengers from freight by the time the first timetable was published in 1852. From 1871 the southern terminus became Ditton Junction. The LNW introduced steam railmotors on the service in 1911 but they proved inadequate for the task and thereafter the line was usually worked by push-pull train sets. Passenger numbers declined after WWI in the face of economic decline and bus competition and the route closed in 1951 when there were just six return trips daily.

Table 154 ST. HELENS, WIDNES, and DITTON JUNCTION (Third class only)

Miles	HOUR (W'k Days, am … pm)	E 6	U 6	8	S 12	S 1		E 4	E 5	5
—	St. Helens Shaw St. dep	20	47	25	42	15	.	37	20	56
¾	Peasley Cross	22	.	27	44	17	.	[illegible]	22	58
1½	Sutton Oak	25	51	29	46	19	.	41	24	**0**
2¾	Clock Face	30	56	33	50	23	.	45	28	4
4¼	Union Bank Farm	34	.	37	54	27	.	49	32	8
5½	Farnworth and Bold	38	**3**	40	57	30	.	52	36	12
6½	Appleton	41	6	43	**0**	33	.	55	39	15
7	Ann Street	44	.	46	3	36	.	58	42	18
7¼	Widnes	47	12	49	6	39	.	**1**	45	21
9	Ditton Junction arr	51	20	56	12	43	.	11	50	26

Miles	HOUR (W'k Days, am … pm)	E 7	U 8	S 12	S 1	E 4	E 5	5	E 6
—	Ditton Junction dep	0	0	15	32	10	.	[illegible]	8
1¾	Widnes	3	7	18	37	16	8	[illegible]	11
2	Ann Street	5	.	20	39	18	9	35	13
2¾	Appleton	8	11	23	42	21	[illegible]	[illegible]	16
3¾	Farnworth and Bold	11	15	26	45	24	[illegible]	41	19
4¾	Union Bank Farm	14	.	29	48	27	.	44	22
6¼	Clock Face	18	22	33	52	31	[illegible]	48	26
7¾	Sutton Oak	22	26	37	56	36	26	52	31
8¼	Peasley Cross	24	.	39	58	38	28	54	33
9	St. Helens Shaw St. arr	28	31	43	**2**	42	36	58	37

E Except Saturdays.
S Saturdays only.
U 1st and 3rd class except on Saturdays

For **OTHER TRAINS** between St. Helens and Sutton Oak, see Table 153a — Widnes and Ditton Junction, Table 138.

March 1951, the year of closing.

Future Plans

On 18th November 2021 the Integrated Rail Plan (IRP) was published, setting out the UK Government's current proposals to transform the rail network in the North and Midlands. Two of the primary projects are the construction of HS2 Phase 2b from Crewe to Manchester, and the delivery of Northern Powerhouse Rail (NPR) with Liverpool – Manchester – Leeds at its core.

With respect to the routes covered by this volume the Fidlers Ferry line will play a key role. Express services from an enhanced and expanded Liverpool Lime Street will feed into the high-speed network via this route, which will be upgraded and electrified, calling at a re-opened Warrington Bank Quay Low Level. Beyond there will be 13 or so miles of new high-speed railway towards Manchester Airport, where London services will join HS2 southbound. NPR trains will continue via the planned HS2 tunnel to Manchester Piccadilly before taking a further new high-speed route as far as Marsden, west of Huddersfield, where they will rejoin the existing network.

Liverpool will therefore not have a dedicated high-speed line and this decision has caused disappointment locally. Because of the scale of the proposals the IRP offers no timeline for completion, but it has been estimated HS2 Phase 2b will not be delivered until 2035-40.

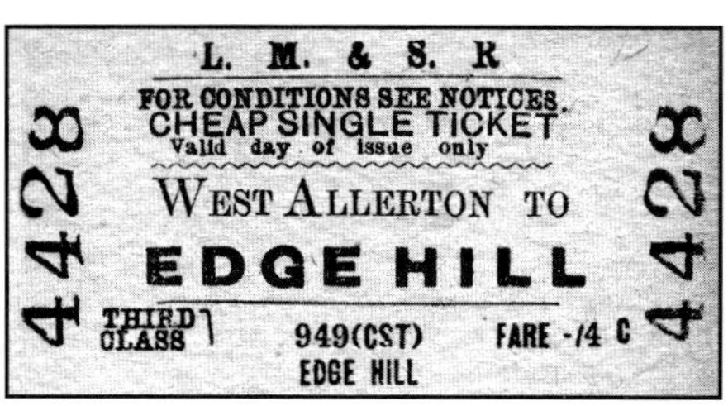

1. Liverpool Lime Street – Runcorn – Sutton Weaver

LIVERPOOL LIME STREET

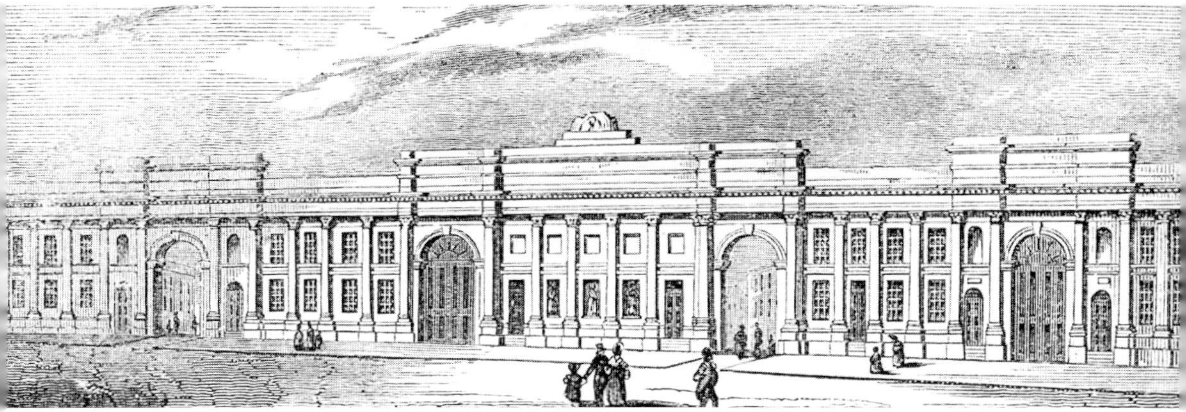

1. We first inspect the station frontage before going inside. This was the impressive entrance to the original station, part funded by Liverpool Corporation, and which stood from 1839 until the commencement of rebuilding in 1869. The illustrator gives us a view through the two open arches of the platform buildings, departures to the left and arrivals right, although not of the station roof. (R.Humm coll.)

2. The caption to this print says Lime Street Station, but it is actually the North Western Hotel which fronted the station's northern trainshed. The hotel opened in 1871 and was the last word in comfort, a stop on the journey to (or from) North America for many of its clientele. It was owned by the LNW and its style is described as French Renaissance. Its fortunes changed after WWI and it closed in 1933. After that it had a variety of uses including offices and student accommodation. It was listed Grade II in 1952. In early 2022 it was being re-converted to a hotel. The picture pre-dates the electrification of the tram system which began in 1898. (Hudson/R.Humm coll.)

Institution
BROWNLOW STREET
PEMBROKE
PEMBROKE GDNS.
Corporation Yard
Timber Yard
County Labory.
PEMBROKE STREET
S.A. Temple
DUCKINFIELD STREET
GREAT NEWTON STREET
Timber Yard
Meat Market
GREAT ORFORD STREET
GILL STREET
Hide, Skin, & Fat Market
Hide & Skin Mart
Hide, Skin, & Fat Market
SHANNON STREET
COPPERAS HILL
Slaughter House
ANDREW STREET
Flour Mill
MOOR PLACE
North End Abattoir
South End Abattoir
LEANDER STREET
Church
BITTERN STREET
MARQUIS ST.
TROWBRIDGE STREET
TROWBRIDGE PL.
POMONA STREET
JERVIS PLACE
JERVIS STREET
BRONTE STREET
TRAFALGAR ST.
TRAFALGAR PL.
GREEK STREET
CLARENCE STREET
PUPIL TEACHERS' COLLEGE
School
RUSSELL STREET
HART STREET
Police Stn.
BK. RUSSELL ST.
RUSSELL PLACE
SEYMOUR STREET
T.C.
BARTLAM ST.
BROWN STREET
EDWARD STREET
JONES STREET
SEGRAVE STREET
TONG STREET
PLEASANT STREET
School
VILLARS STREET
GLOUCESTER ST.
Church
ROCK STREET
MAY STREET
ST. VINCENT ST.
ST. VINCENT STREET
AINSWORTH STREET
WARREN STREET
HARFORD STREET
BRIDPORT STREET
Tobacco Works
Tobacco Works
MARY ANN ST.
BLAKE STREET
HAWKE STREET
R.C. Pro Cathedral
Presby.
Hall
School
MOUNT
LORD NELSON STREET
HOTHAM STREET
HOTHAM ST.
Midland Adelphi Hotel
UPPER NEWINGTON
Hotel
Central Hall
Hall
The Stadium
Lime Street Station (Terminus)
HILBRE STREET
Wand Bdy.
SKELHORNE STREET
Empire Theatre
BOLTON STREET
Cinema
Cinema
RANELAGH PLACE
CROPPER STREET
LAWTON STREET
Central Station
North Western Hotel
DISLEY ST.
GLOUCESTER ST.
LIME STREET
Cinema
Statue
FAIRCLOUGH ST.
ST. GEORGE'S PLACE
Hotel St. George
ST. GEORGE'S HALL
St. John's Wholesale Fish Market
ROSE STREET
ELLIOT STREET
DEANE STREET
Bank
RANELAGH STREET
Lyceum
St. John's Fish Market
GREAT CHARLOTTE STREET
OASES STREET
Cinema
ST. JOHN'S GARDEN
Royal Court Theatre
St. John's Market (Meat, Fruit, Vegetables &c.)
CLAYTON SQUARE
WATERLOO PLACE
ST. JOHN'S LANE
QUEEN SQUARE
ROE STREET
MARKET STREET
HOUGHTON STREET
PARKER ST.
Bank
Stork Hotel
UPPER DAWSON ST.
Playhouse Theatre
TYRER STREET
BRYTHEN ST.

III. The map is dated 1924. The station's overall roof obscures the platforms and interior trackwork, but we can locate two turntables and the signal box beneath the 'H' of Copperas Hill.

Lime Street is one of Britain's most famous railway stations, although it is not Liverpool's oldest. It was authorised on 23rd May 1832 to replace the inconveniently sited Crown Street terminus of the pioneering L&M and opened on 15th August 1836. The extension descended from Edge Hill through a tunnel at 1:83/93. This was cable worked until 1870.

Lime Street itself is said to have taken its name from lime kilns that operated on the fringe of the town in the 18th century. The Corporation of Liverpool used the arrival of the railway to create a major civic square, with the station on the east side of Lime Street, and St George's Hall, completed in 1854, on its west side.

The station initially consisted of two platforms, one for arrivals, the other for departures, either side of carriage sidings. There was an overall roof, believed to have been the first train shed in the world. Trains initially ran only to Manchester, but from 4th July 1837 the Grand Junction Railway linked Liverpool with Birmingham, and from 24th June 1838 rail travel to London began.

The station was first extended to cope with growing traffic between 1846-49, during which the original trackside buildings were lost. It was enlarged a second time between 1867-79 to reach its existing size. The familiar twin elliptical roofs 620ft long and 385ft wide in total were constructed at this time. The northern shed covered the site of the original station and was designed by the LNW's Chief Engineer William Baker and completed in 1869; the southern shed was added between 1874-79. All subsequent alterations have been within this footprint. The number of platforms has varied, but with a maximum of 11. All lines were electrified in 1961. The fabric of the entire station was listed Grade II in 1975.

During 2017-18 the station underwent its biggest upgrade since the 1870s at a cost of £340m. In summary, the track was removed from platform 1; platforms 2-7 were renumbered 1-6; new platforms 7 & 8 replaced the old cab road; platforms 8 & 9 were renumbered 9 & 10; the platforms were generally widened; and platforms 1 & 2 and 9 & 10 were lengthened. The remodelled station reopened after a 16-day closure on 30th July 2018. The 10 platforms are now equally distributed between the two trainsheds, and normally the northern shed is used by services towards Huyton, and the southern shed by those towards Liverpool South Parkway, thus reducing conflicting movements.

3. The extreme left of this busy scene very slightly overlaps the right of the previous image. It shows the south trainshed with the carriage drive at left. The electric tram, on the Pier Head – Knotty Ash route, is the only vehicle in view which is not horse drawn. Estimated date 1903. (P.Laming coll.)

4. This view dates from 29th April 2014 and is comparable with no. 3 on the previous page. A corner of the erstwhile hotel is just visible at left, beyond which we see a small portion of the northern trainshed roof. But the main feature is the southern trainshed. All the premises that stood in front of it were swept away in 2009 and replaced by flights of steps, opening up a fine vista both inward and outward. (A C.Hartless)

5. The remainder of our study is of the station's interior. This splendid view of the northern trainshed is entitled 'Lime Street Station, Liverpool, at the end of the 19th century'. From right to left we see platforms 2-6. Platform 1 is obscured by empty stock in the siding between platforms 1 & 2 at the right. There is another carriage siding between platforms 3 & 4, and two shorter ones between 5 & 6. The trains at platforms 4 & 6 appear to be headed by LNW 2-4-0s, whilst those at nos 2 & 5 have tank engines. This track layout remained with little alteration until the refurbishment of 2018. (*The Railway Magazine*/R.Humm coll.)

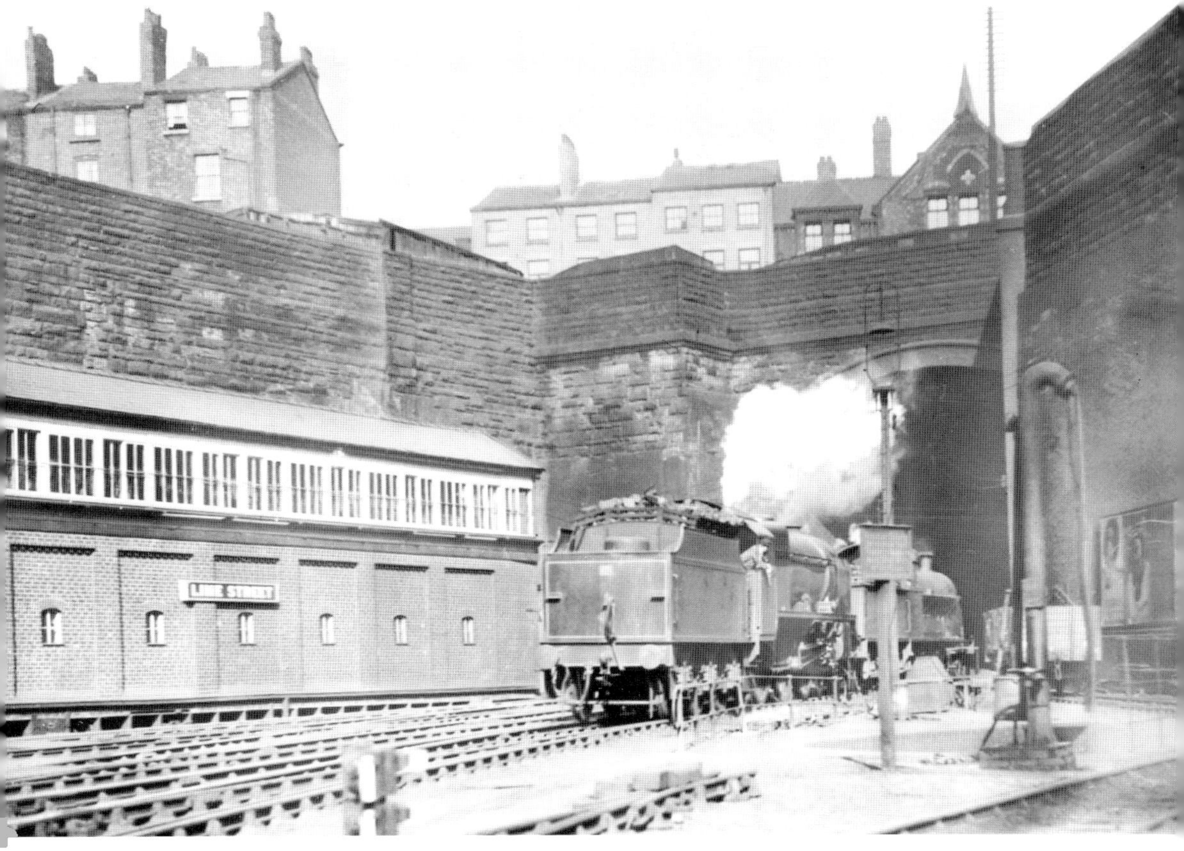

6. This early 1930s view of LMS Royal Scot 4-6-0 no. 6132 *Phoenix* and an LNW Prince of Wales 4-6-0 backing onto an express departing from the southern trainshed features the impressive LNW signal box, which stood between the tracks at the station's throat. Built in 1877 and extended in 1885 (when the line to Edge Hill was quadrupled) and again in 1907, it ultimately had 155 levers. It closed on 25th January 1948. (D.Ibbotson/R.S.Carpenter coll.)

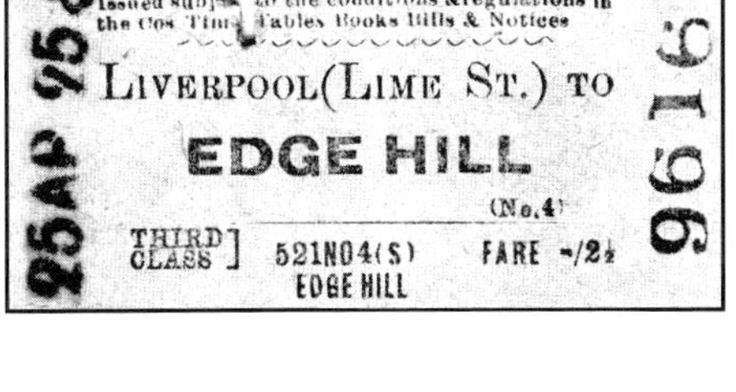

7. No book covering the Lime Street/Edge Hill area would be complete without several contributions from The Right Reverend Bishop Eric Treacy, who was Vicar of Edge Hill from 1936-40 and a railway photographer par excellence for far longer. He never dated his photos, but circa 1953 would be a good guess for this shot of Jubilee 4-6-0 no. 45646 *Napier* leaving platform 5 on what he describes on the back of the hand-printed image as 'a train for Hull'. Shot from the lineside the loco has just passed beneath Copperas Hill bridge, leaving the northern trainshed full of smoke. (E.Treacy/R.Humm coll.)

For further views of Liverpool, see: *Liverpool Tramways (1.The Eastern Routes)*, *Liverpool Tramways (2.The Southern Routes)* **and** *Liverpool Tramways (3.The Northern Routes)*.

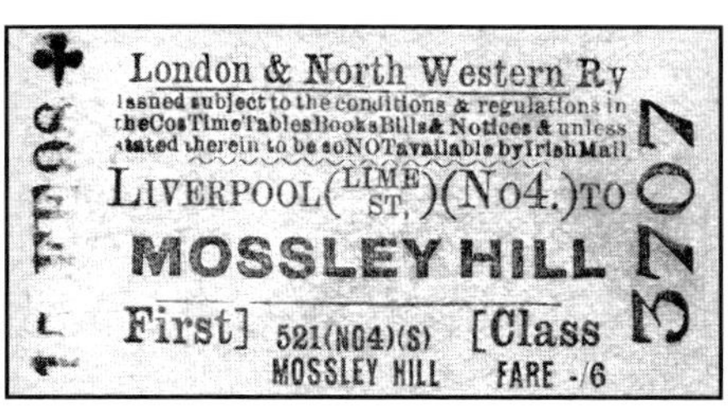

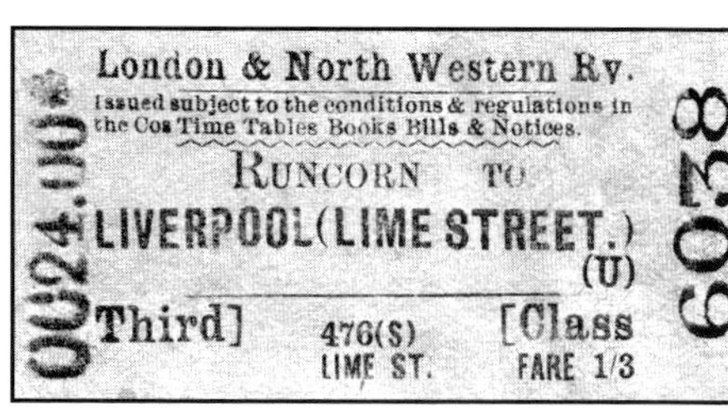

8. Here is a fine view of the southern trainshed from 16th June 1963. 8P 4-6-2 no. 46240 *City of Coventry* stands at platform 8 with an afternoon relief service to London Euston. One has to look a long way to the right to see a train in platform 7, behind the parked cars on the cab road. At far left are platforms 10 & 11, looking quiet and which were decommissioned in 1969; the space was given over to road vehicles, eg Royal Mail. Note also the pile of mailbags and the youngster on platform 9 admiring the big maroon engine. (J.Corkill/8D Association)

9. The photographer is standing at the end of platform 10 to record Britannia Pacific no. 70004, originally *William Shakespeare*. Beyond it is the final Liverpool Lime Street signal box, an LMS electro-mechanical design that replaced the box seen in picture 6. It served until 13th July 2018 after which its duties passed to the Manchester Railway Operating Centre (ROC). Behind the loco is the south side turntable, which was dismantled after the end of steam. The date of the photo is 4th June 1966. The loco is awaiting the arrival from Euston of 'The Fellsman', an LCGB railtour that the Pacific worked forward to Carlisle. (Great Western Trust)

10. On 18th November 2018 we see the remodelled southern trainshed. TransPennine Express (TPE) liveried no. 68019 *Brutus* departs from the new platform 7 with a light engine crew training run to Crewe. A class 156 DMU stands at platform 8. Platforms 9 & 10 are to its left whilst platform 6, usually the preserve of the hourly fast London Euston service, is the opposite face to platform 7. Comparison with picture no. 8 shows how platforms 7 & 8 occupy the space previously taken by the cab road. (D.Birmingham/8D Association)

11. On 28th November 2019 we see the remodelled northern trainshed. TPE Nova1 bi-mode unit no. 802203 stands at platform 1, formerly no. 2, with the 10.25 to Newcastle. This platform was extended from 162m to 220m from 14th October 2018, the last act of the 2017-18 upgrade. To its right we see first the train crew depot, a couple of non-descript office and mess buildings which stand close to the site of the north side turntable. Next comes the end of the trackless former platform 1, now known as platform 0. An elderly class 142 Pacer unit stands at platform 3, and nearly new Civity emu no. 331112 occupies platform 5 with a Wigan service. (J.Whitehouse)

IV. This extract is derived from a 6ins to 1 mile map, dated 1925. Our route from Lime Street to Edge Hill was originally in tunnel and the map shows the extent to which that was subsequently opened out, e.g. above Chatham Place near the left-hand margin. On the north side of the station the Waterloo Dock branch emerges from its tunnel, and on the south side the Park Lane (aka Wapping) branch accessed Crown Street (adjacent to Smithdown Lane) and the southern docks. Our route, the Edge Hill & Garston Line, leaves the four-track L&M line below the word Gridirons and runs beneath two goods lines; between them it passes Edge Hill locoshed on the up side. The section between Edge Hill no. 3 signal box and Wavertree Junction, around ½ mile, is the only stretch of the Lime Street – Ditton route never to have been quadrupled.

When the L&M opened, the section from Crown Street to Edge Hill was cable worked; steam haulage took over thence to Manchester. Edge Hill was therefore a stopping place out of necessity. When Lime Street replaced Crown Street, Edge Hill was once again the change-over point between steam and cable traction, at a point slightly north of the original. The two-storey passenger buildings that still stand on the opposite platforms date from the 1836 deviation. The station is thus one of the oldest in the world to retain its original buildings. The Waterloo Dock branch opened on 1st August 1849. This also was cable worked and the opportunity was taken to provide new winding gear for the Wapping and Lime Street inclines.

Following the end of cable working to Lime Street in 1870 the tunnel thence was opened out as far as practicable to aid ventilation. Between 1885-89 the route was quadrupled, a challenging task through the sandstone whilst maintaining services. It was at this point that the number of through platforms at Edge Hill increased from two to four and the station was further enlarged by the addition of two east facing bays in the north platform primarily for services to Alexandra and Canada Docks. This era was the high-water mark for Edge Hill station, with virtually all trains including London expresses calling.

After 1900 custom diminished as trams and then buses provided more convenient door to door journeys for many. Thankfully, the historic buildings survived the modernisation plan that accompanied the Crewe – Liverpool electrification, and they received grade II/II* listed status in 1974. Demographics and the hollowing out of inner-city employment, not least on the railway itself, further eroded passenger numbers, which stood at a modest 162,000 for 2019-20 (Office of Rail & Road) compared to 16 million at Lime Street. The casual visitor in the early 2020s may well form an impression of an interesting outdoor museum as much as a useful passenger interchange.

But Edge Hill's railway history has been about much more than passengers. Its strategic position atop the sandstone ridge and, until the later 19th century, on the outskirts of the city made it ripe for the development of vast sorting sidings for goods to and from the docks, also three goods stations, two sets of carriage sidings, a wagon repair depot, and a major locomotive shed.

12. This fascinating engraving is entitled 'Edge Hill station, Liverpool, 1848 (L&NW Railway)'. The train has been hauled by rope from Lime Street, and the unidentified 2-2-2 has coupled up for the onward journey. The elegant trainshed was replaced by canopies at some point, but the tunnel mouth can be seen again in picture 14 whilst the up side building reappears 156 years later in picture 18. (A.F.Tait/SSPL)

13. The subject of this photo of circa 1930 is LMS 3F 0-6-0T no. 16487 shunting the sidings serving the Waterloo Dock line. This was one of a batch of 50 of this large class built by Vulcan Foundry in 1926, and it became no. 7404 under the LMS 1934 renumbering scheme. It was withdrawn from Edge Hill shed in 1962 and may well have spent its entire life based there. Edge Hill station, seen from the north-east, is in the background. We can see the greater part of platform 1 and its lengthy canopy. This rests against a tall wall supporting the overall roof that covered the bay platforms; a rake of coaches is parked in the more northerly one. We can see the start of the platform 2 canopy, and to its left the lower canopy covering platforms 3 and 4. Beyond that is more coaching stock in the carriage shed yard. (Real Photographs/R.Humm coll.)

14. On 27th June 1959 8P 4-6-2 no. 46203 *Princess Margaret Rose* emerges from the 58 yards of Tunnel Road Tunnel en route for London Euston with 'The Merseyside Express'. It is reaching the top of the climb from Lime Street and is passing platform 2, the original departure platform. Change was afoot; the first batch of English Electric Type 4 diesels for the West Coast Main Line was in the process of delivery and would soon begin to sideline the Princess Royal Pacifics. Also, the track through platform 2 would soon alter from the up fast line to the down slow under the electrification scheme. (P.H.Hanson)

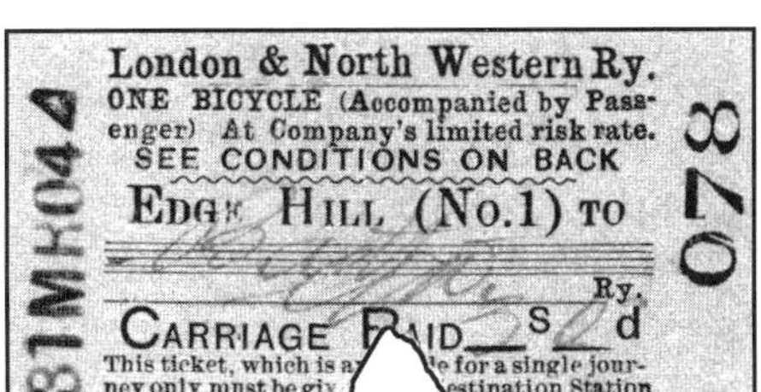

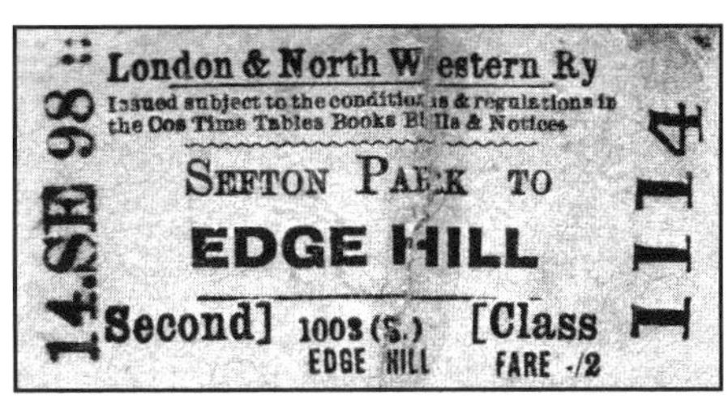

15. This extra passenger train was recorded in May 1966 running through platform 3. This was the down fast line until the Edge Hill area was re-signalled in 1960 when it became the up fast. The loco is Britannia Pacific no. 70021, formerly *Morning Star*, and working from Stockport shed. We can see from left to right: the long canopy covering platforms 3 & 4, part of the seven-road carriage shed, the parcels lift and bridge, none of which exist today. (J.Corkill/8D Association)

16. This view east from 14th January 1977 shows nos. 24133 and 24082 running light through platform 3 to the loco holding sidings. The scene is desolate; only two short stretches of canopy remain, the remainder having been dismantled. The parcels bridge has been removed, leaving the lift shaft isolated. The temporary palings suggest that it and the walls behind the locos will shortly be demolished. The carriage sidings are still active with Mark 1 stock in view. (T.Heavyside)

17. The demolition of the carriage shed opened up a new north-easterly view of the station from Tunnel Road. On 12th January 1991 no. 86233 *Laurence Olivier* runs through platform 4 with the 11.40 Euston – Lime Street and passes the rear of the southern range of the station buildings. The course of the Park Lane branch is evident on the right. (D.Birmingham/8D Association)

18. The historic station buildings were restored as closely as possible to their original appearance by 1979, with all canopies and accoutrements removed. The range on the northern platform is seen on 24th June 2004. We are looking north-west from the southern platform. At the extreme left is the approach road, itself listed along with its walls, down from Tunnel Road. Next comes the two-storey station building in red sandstone; the entrance door is out of view on its far end. The sympathetic extension was built to cover the stairwell to the underground passage linking the platforms. The flat-roofed tower is the winding house of 1849. The buildings nearest the camera are the hydraulic plant house and accumulator tower built in 1882 to serve the Gridiron marshalling yard. (A.C.Hartless)

EAST OF EDGE HILL

At the height of the LNW's growth the L&M east of Edge Hill was surrounded by sidings and depots that lasted beyond the end of the steam age.

19. A classic Eric Treacy shot from 1936 features LMS 8P 4-6-2 no. 6201 *Princess Elizabeth* with 'The Merseyside Express', the 10.10 Lime Street to Euston, the principal morning service between Liverpool and London. The rear of the train is just clearing the station, and we see Edge Hill No. 2 signal box on the left; this served from 1887 to 1947 when it was replaced by a new box, which lasted until 1961. It was also known as Lime Street Junction, ie the point of divergence of the 1836 line to Lime Street from the 1830 line to Crown Street. Edge Hill Power Signal Box (PSB) was opened on 28th August 1961, beyond the left of this view, when electric colour lights replaced semaphore signals. To the right is Edge Hill Goods, with a Jinty shunting in the middle of the wagons. This closed in May 1972.
(E.Treacy/R.Humm coll.)

➔ 20. This is the view east from Picton Road bridge on 12th June 1959. The train is the 7.45 Euston – Lime Street, which judging by its short length has divided from a longer train at Crewe, hauled by 8P 4-6-2 no. 46209 *Princess Beatrice*. The building at track level at the extreme left is the wagon repair works. A short distance away a Jinty is attached to a long line of vans in the lower Gridiron. Another string of vans occupies one of the roads in Tuebrook Sidings in the middle of the picture. In the mid-distance is Edge Hill No. 3 signal box, also known as Garston Junction. This served from 1882-1961 and controlled the four-track main line and the junctions towards both Wavertree and Bootle. To the right of the train are the goods lines from Wapping, which climb in the background to Viaduct Junction, marked by the tall Edge Hill No. 4 signal box and three-armed signal. The track branching to the right edge of the picture is leading to Downhill Carriage Sidings and the track coming in from the right is from Spekeland Road Goods. (B.Brooksbank/*Wikimedia Commons*)

↓ 21. The photographer has captured the view westwards in the later 1950s from Viaduct Junction adjacent to Edge Hill No. 4 signal box. This served from 1887-1969. In the foreground is the four-tracked L&M line. Trailing into the left-hand line is the single-track lead from Edge Hill locoshed, and beyond that the two tracks going off to the left are our route to Wavertree and the south. Patriot 4-6-0 no. 45542 is getting a train of empty mineral wagons for St Helens underway from Tuebrook Sidings. These and the Gridiron fell out of use in the early 1980s and the area was redeveloped. (Rail Online)

← 22. Our intrepid photographer is standing on the bridge carrying the Wavertree Junction – Engine Shed Junction high-level goods line across the Edge Hill & Garston sometime in the early 1950s. He has recorded 5MT 4-6-0 no. 45418 barking up the 1:93 gradient past Edge Hill locoshed with a mixed consist of carriages including at least four ex-GWR vehicles. This suggests a Lime Street to Bristol service, maybe via Birmingham New Street as the loco was a long-term Aston resident. To the left are Downhill Carriage Sidings and to the right 8A's mechanical coaling plant where a WD 2-8-0 is shunting wagon loads of loco coal. We note the manicured edge to the ballast on the main line. (*Yoliverpool.com*)

Edge Hill Locoshed

The L&M had rudimentary loco servicing facilities at Edge Hill from the start, it being the end of the line for locomotive working. This soon took the form of covered accommodation and workshops on the south side of the line adjacent to Lime Street Junction. The LNW realised it would need enlarged facilities when the Edge Hill – Garston route opened, and its new locoshed was built soon afterwards. The nearest open country in 1864 was south of the L&M line immediately east of Garston Junction. The shed was spacious with 20 straight roads of 200ft. Nevertheless the level of traffic required more accommodation by the end of the century and in 1902 a 12 road shed was added at the north-east end of the original. The depot was one of the first to receive a mechanical coaling plant, in 1914, at which time around 140 locomotives were allocated here, ranging from express passenger types to dockyard shunters. In 1959 it was reckoned the shed employed some 700 railwaymen and women. It was coded number 26 by the LNW, and 8A from 1935 which it retained until it closed to steam from 6th May 1968 only three months before the end of steam on BR. It was soon demolished, leaving a small diesel servicing depot constructed in the mid-1960s.

23. The shadows show this line up of express steam power was taken at the shed's west end, and the date is most likely the summer of 1953, when no. 46138 *The London Irish Rifleman* was allocated to 1B Camden. At left is no. 46115 *Scots Guardsman* from 9A Longsight, destined to be the last working Royal Scot when withdrawn at the end of 1965 whereupon it was secured for preservation. Centre stage is no. 46208 *Princess Helena Victoria*, which was shedded here from mid-1951 until withdrawal in October 1962. Note the water cranes, one to every two roads. (E.Treacy/R.Humm coll.)

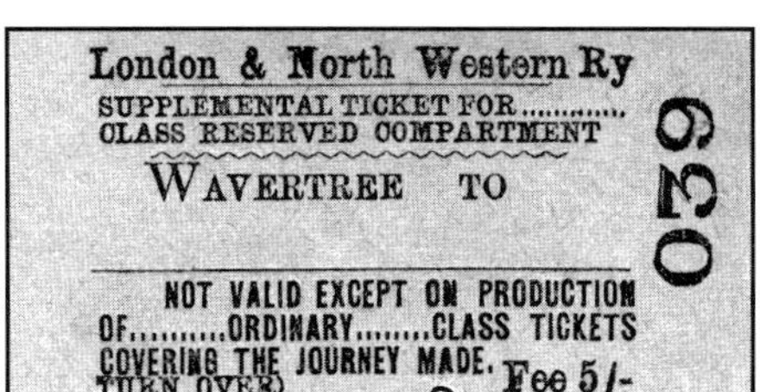

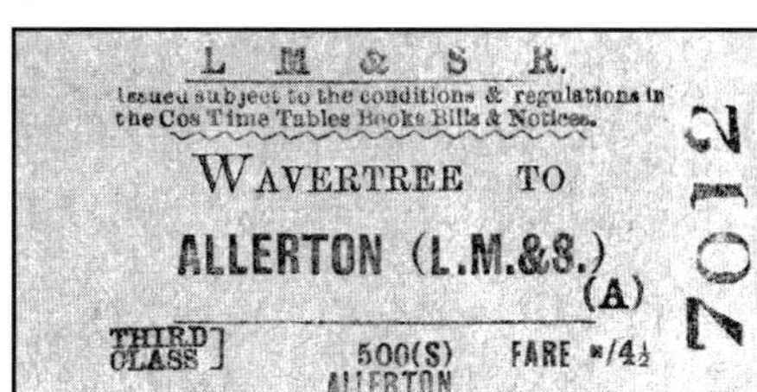

NORTH OF WAVERTREE
Wavertree Junction

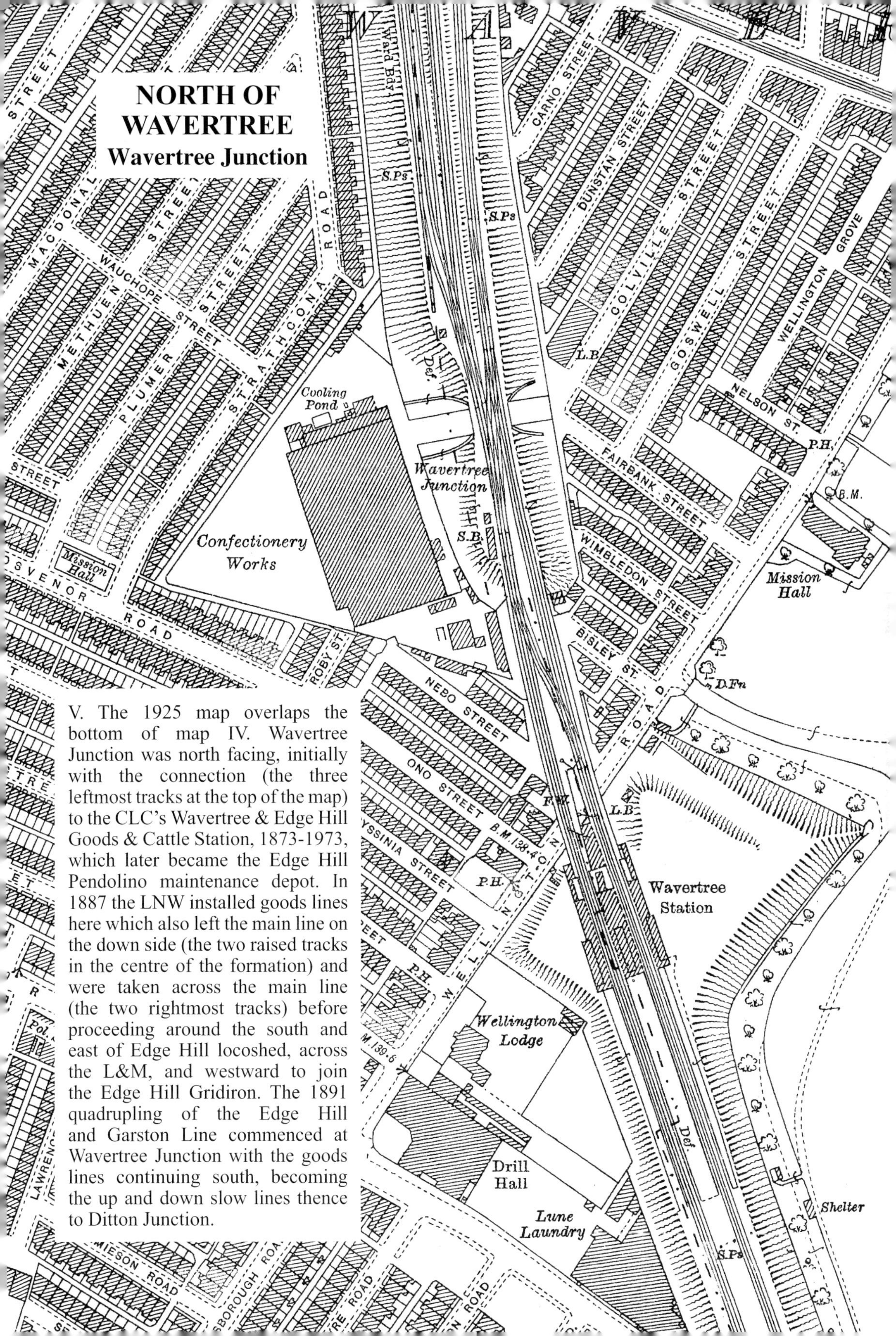

V. The 1925 map overlaps the bottom of map IV. Wavertree Junction was north facing, initially with the connection (the three leftmost tracks at the top of the map) to the CLC's Wavertree & Edge Hill Goods & Cattle Station, 1873-1973, which later became the Edge Hill Pendolino maintenance depot. In 1887 the LNW installed goods lines here which also left the main line on the down side (the two raised tracks in the centre of the formation) and were taken across the main line (the two rightmost tracks) before proceeding around the south and east of Edge Hill locoshed, across the L&M, and westward to join the Edge Hill Gridiron. The 1891 quadrupling of the Edge Hill and Garston Line commenced at Wavertree Junction with the goods lines continuing south, becoming the up and down slow lines thence to Ditton Junction.

24. On 12th October 1957 the prototype *Deltic* approaches Wavertree Junction with a Lime Street – Euston express. The train is cresting the summit of the 1:93 climb from Edge Hill No. 3 and is passing beneath the Wavertree Junction – Engine Shed Junction goods line. (J.A.Peden/8D Association)

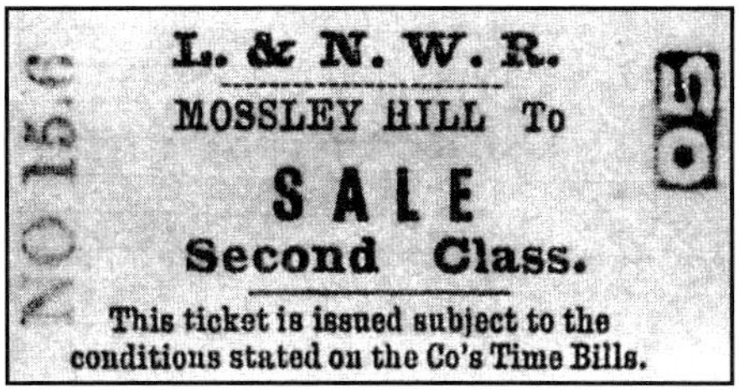

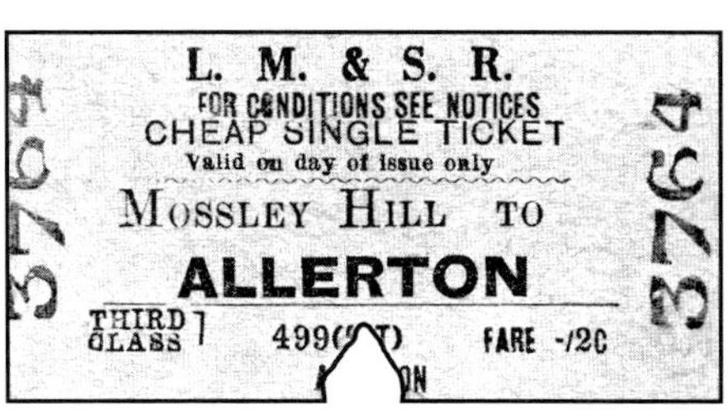

WAVERTREE

The station was a little less than 1¼ miles from Edge Hill. It opened on 1st September 1870 in response to urban development. From 13th July 1891 it was enlarged from two to four platforms when the quadrupling took effect. Thereafter it remained in much the same condition until it closed from 5th August 1958 due to lack of patronage, local buses being far more frequent.

↗ 25. This stirring sight appears to be an LNW Lime Street – Euston express of c1900 accelerating on the falling gradient of the up main. The pilot loco is no. 3020 *Cornwall* and the train engine is an LNW 2-4-0. *Cornwall* was a unique engine, built as long ago as 1847 as a 4-2-2 but subsequently converted to 2-2-2 and further modified, most recently in 1887, to the form seen here. The driving wheels were a massive 8ft 6ins. It was withdrawn by 1907 and preserved at Crewe Works, its birthplace. It was returned to work c1913 hauling the Chief Mechanical Engineer's saloon and was finally retired in 1930 after taking part in the L&M centenary. In 2022 it could be found on display at the Buckinghamshire Rly Centre at Quainton Road. (*Disused-stations.org.uk*)

↓ 26. Wavertree station seems to have been little photographed. This image was taken in 1958 shortly before closure and site clearance. A Stanier 3MT 2-6-2T is approaching the up slow platform causing Standard 5MT 4-6-0 no. 73099 of Patricroft to be held by signals on the down main. Wavertree Junction signal box is dimly visible in the left background; this closed in 1961 when its area came under the control of the new Edge Hill PSB. We get a sense of the timber platform structures and canopies, also the staircase linking the central island platform with the small booking office on Wellington Road. (Stations UK)

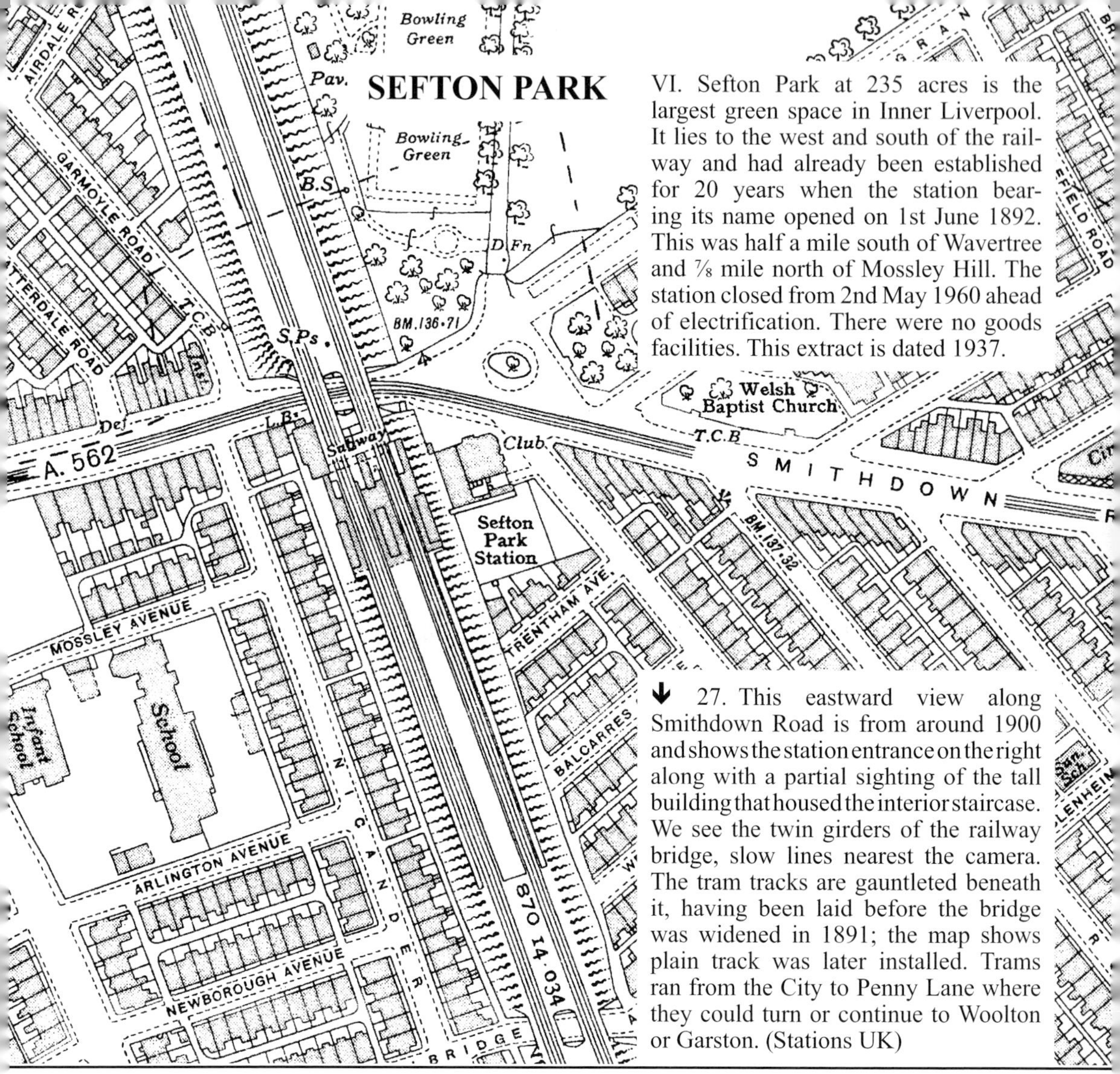

VI. Sefton Park at 235 acres is the largest green space in Inner Liverpool. It lies to the west and south of the railway and had already been established for 20 years when the station bearing its name opened on 1st June 1892. This was half a mile south of Wavertree and ⅞ mile north of Mossley Hill. The station closed from 2nd May 1960 ahead of electrification. There were no goods facilities. This extract is dated 1937.

↓ 27. This eastward view along Smithdown Road is from around 1900 and shows the station entrance on the right along with a partial sighting of the tall building that housed the interior staircase. We see the twin girders of the railway bridge, slow lines nearest the camera. The tram tracks are gauntleted beneath it, having been laid before the bridge was widened in 1891; the map shows plain track was later installed. Trams ran from the City to Penny Lane where they could turn or continue to Woolton or Garston. (Stations UK)

28. This picture shows little of the station infrastructure, but it does illustrate an up express, most likely the 5.25pm to Euston, circa August 1949. It is hauled by 8P 4-6-2 no. 46202, a regular visitor to Merseyside, which was built in 1935 as an experimental turbine driven steam loco and soon earned the sobriquet 'the Turbomotive'. It was taken out of traffic in May 1950 and rebuilt as a conventionally driven loco, only to be damaged beyond economic repair in the Harrow collision of 8th October 1952 after less than two months of service. (J.E.Connor coll.)

29. The station is not known to have altered much during its 68 years and is seen here at platform level in 1958 as a Patriot 4-6-0 runs along the up fast line with a local passenger service. The structures are strikingly similar to Allerton's, see picture 36. (Stations UK)

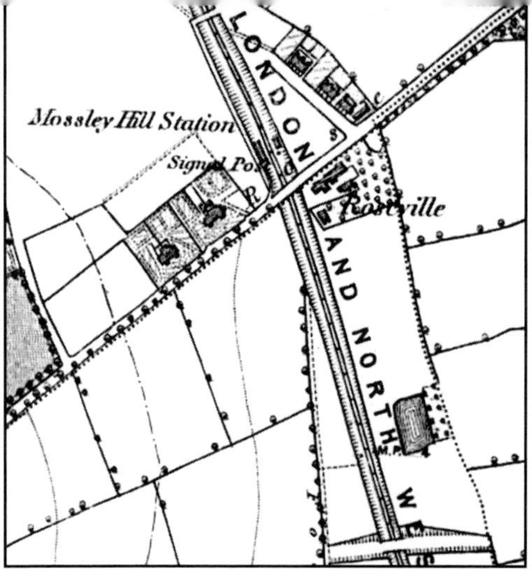

MOSSLEY HILL

VII. The station, 2¼ miles from Edge Hill, opened with the line in an area of scattered villas and market gardens. The first station was on the north side of Rose Lane (inset, left). It was relocated to its present site on the south side of Rose Lane from 13th July 1891 because of the quadrupling of the route which took effect 4½ months later. The original signal box was an integral part of the old station and was replaced by a new box south of the second station from 22nd September 1891. Four-tracking created two further platforms by converting two side platforms into two islands. Also in 1891 two goods sidings were provided off the down slow line to the south of the station; this facility never had a warehouse, merely a loading dock, and it closed from 7th December 1964. The signal box closed from 6th August 1960 when its functions were taken over by Allerton Junction, and the semaphore signals were replaced by electric colour lights. The station buildings were rebuilt in 1961 ahead of electrification. It was officially called Mossley Hill for Aigburth from around 1880 until 6th May 1974. The main extract is dated 1937; the 6ins to 1 mile inset is dated 1864.

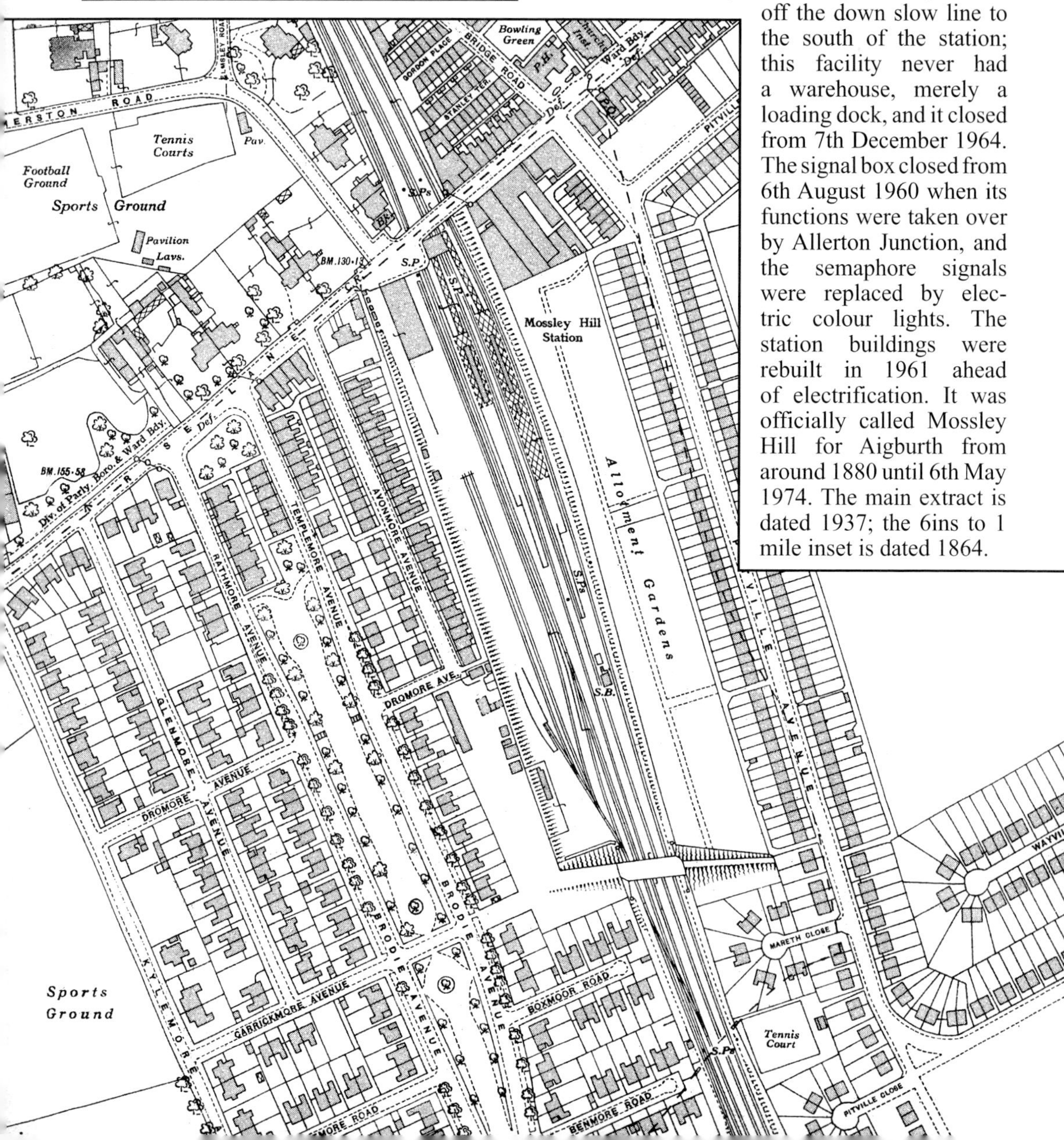

30. *Princess Elizabeth* is seen again, in March 1938, pulling away with the 10.10 Lime Street – Euston. London trains called here until the 1950s. We get a glimpse of the goods yard at left, and the superstructure of the signal box although the train obscures the station. (E.Treacy/6201 Princess Elizabeth Society)

31. This southward view from around 1953 shows the layout that was created by quadrupling, with the fast lines island platform on the left and the slow lines on the right. Between the fast lines is the signal box and across the tracks the view of the goods station is partly obscured by the right-hand platform building. It is apparent that the left-hand building is the larger of the two. (Postcards & Covers)

32. The map shows the four platforms were of differing lengths and there was once a canopy extending roughly to where the photographer later stood. The platform buildings are concentrated at the north end of the platforms and are of standard LNW design of timber construction with hipped slate roofs, brick chimneys and wide canopies. Beyond these we can see covered staircases leading to the street, reached via the booking office at right angles to the track with the exit on its west side protected by a small awning. The ramped roadway on the left linked the goods station with Rose Lane. (Stations UK)

33A. BR's London Midland Region press office issued several pictures of the newly electrified railway including this one of the rebuilt station probably taken in the summer of 1961. Platform 2, the down fast, is the viewpoint and we see a prefabricated shelter typical of the Crewe – Liverpool/Manchester electrification scheme. Here it gleams in the sun but would not prove as durable as its predecessor. We see the staircases have been replaced by open air ramps, and at their tops the roof line of the new booking office is visible. (BR/R.Humm coll.)

33B. There have been few changes since 1961, other than replacing the platform shelters from time to time. By 5th October 1996 brick had replaced timber and glass as no. 60095 *Crib Goch* ran up the slow line with coal from Liverpool Bulk Terminal to Fidlers Ferry… (D.Birmingham/8D Association)

➚ 33C …whilst on 7th November 2016 steel and glass were à la mode as a Pendolino passed with the 12.47 Lime Street – Euston. Note the picket fencing which effectively reduced the platform lengths to 4 vehicles. Passenger usage in 2019-20 was 157,000. (A.C.Hartless)

WEST ALLERTON

VIII. This is ¾ mile from Mossley Hill and 1 mile before Liverpool South Parkway. It was opened by the LMS on 2nd January 1939 in response to the southward spread of Liverpool. The map shows the position in 1937. The area between Mossley Hill and Allerton was rural until the 1920s, when Mather Avenue (off the map) was built roughly parallel to the east of the railway and the tramline to Garston was laid in its central reservation. Housing development followed rapidly. Booker Avenue was originally Booker's Lane, which the railway severed in 1864 when a footbridge was substituted. It was extended eastwards to link with Mather Avenue in 1938, crossing the railway, and the station was built on the south side of the new bridge. There were no goods facilities.

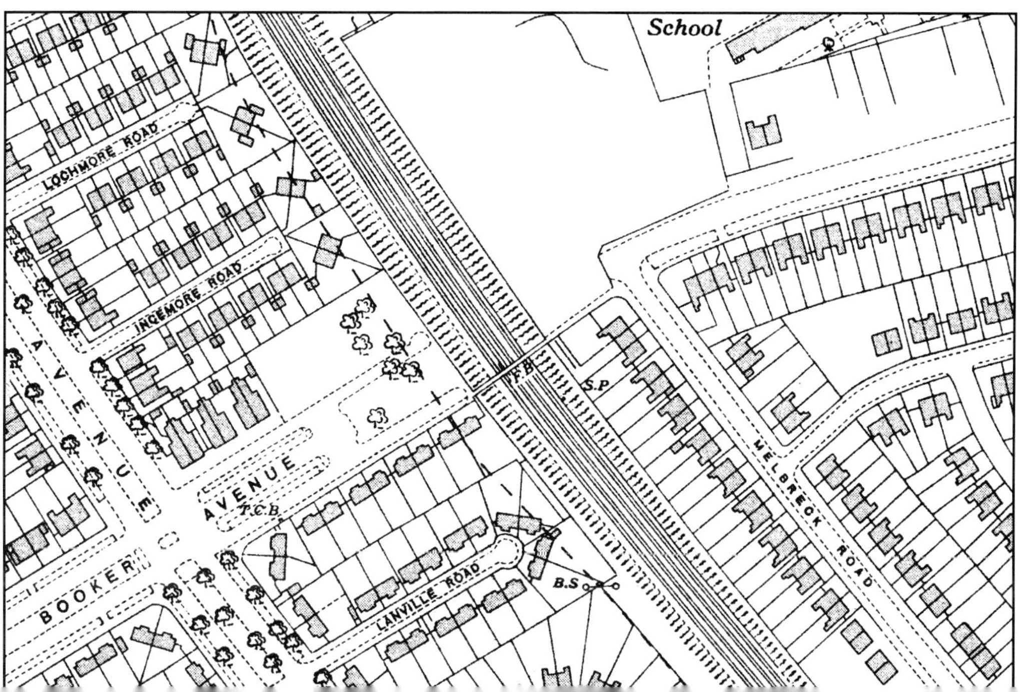

34. This is a southward view from the station footbridge c1959 and shows the station in its original condition except for signage. The modest prefabricated buildings contrast with the larger establishments elsewhere on the line. Note the decorative feature on the up side embankment which had as its centrepiece a plaque ‘Star Turns’ celebrating the named trains that passed here in the 50s and early 60s, ie ‘The Manxman’, ‘The Merseyside Express’, ‘The Red Rose’ and ‘The Shamrock’. (P.Graham/8D Association)

35. This northward image from April 2016 sees EMU no. 319375 passing through the up slow platform, no. 3, with a Lime Street – South Parkway service. These former Thameslink units began to arrive on Merseyside in 2015 when they were already over 25 years old. The platform shelters have been renewed with even smaller modern versions. In the background we see the station footbridge linking the four platforms with the original entrance/booking office at street level above platform 4. Passenger usage in 2019-20 was 55,000. (D.Birmingham)

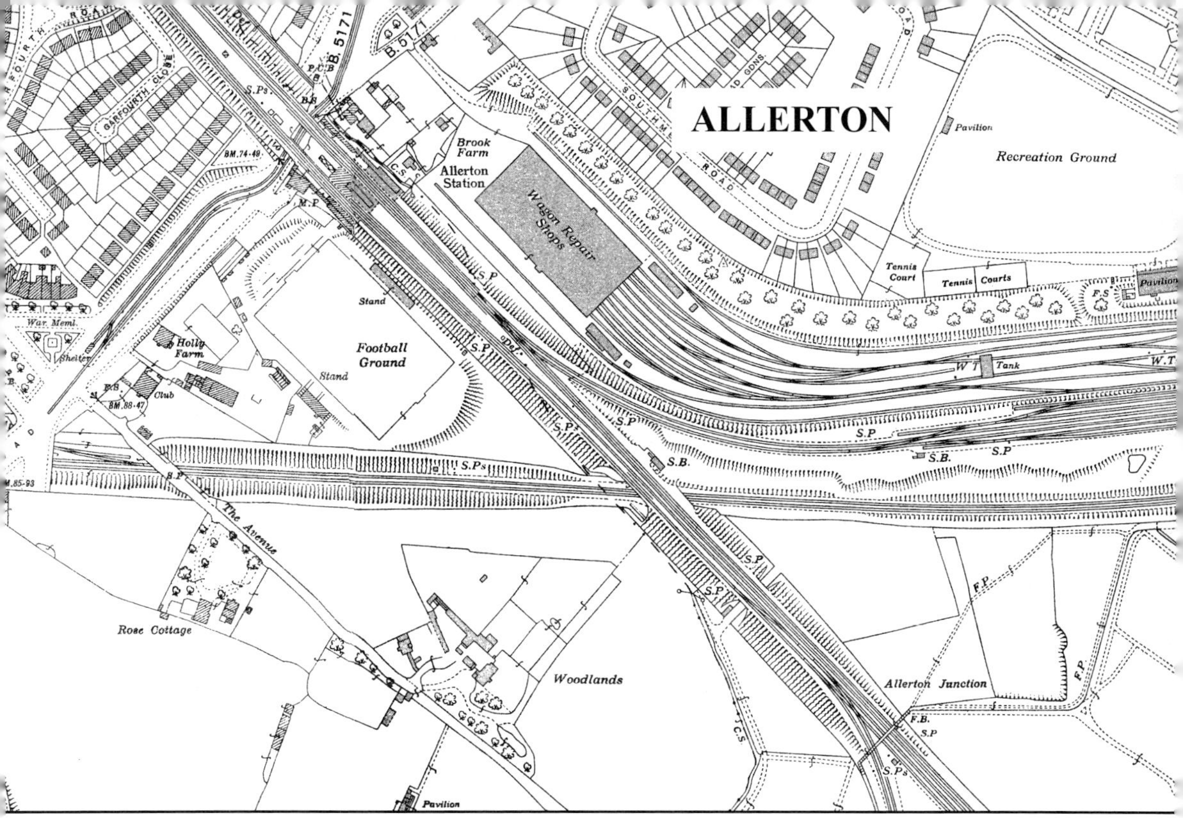

IX. This extract is dated 1937. The station opened with the Edge Hill – Speke Junction line on 15th February 1864. It was located 4¼ miles from Edge Hill where the line crossed the Woolton road half a mile from Garston Dock. The station initially consisted of two side platforms, of which no photographs are known; there were no goods facilities. Allerton was a dispersed rural area that was absorbed by the county borough of Liverpool in 1913.

On 1st January 1873 the Garston Curve opened between Allerton Junction (later Allerton East Junction) and Garston Junction on the former SHCR allowing direct travel between Lime Street and Garston Dock. On 14th May 1873 the CLC (whose main line runs across the map from left to right) opened a curve from Hunts Cross to Allerton to facilitate access to its Wavertree & Edge Hill Goods & Cattle Station. It further opened a locoshed, named Allerton, on the north side of the curve, which was in use from 1882-1897, following which it became a carriage and wagon repair depot.

When the LNW main line was quadrupled between Wavertree Junction and Speke Junction, Allerton station gained two further platforms, despite the lack of any significant house building nearby until the 1920s. The first major development close to the station was the opening in 1909 of the 150-acre Allerton Cemetery, one of the main burial sites for the City of Liverpool. Trams ran along Woolton Road between the mid-1920s and 1953. Picture no. 112 of *Liverpool Tramways vol. 2 The Southern Routes* includes the railway bridge across Woolton Road and the station entrance c1953.

After 1891 there was little change until the advent of the Crewe-Liverpool electrification. The former CLC shed site was chosen for a new Traction Maintenance Depot (TMD) for diesel and electric stock. The lines between Mossley Hill and Woodside and the Garston area were re-signalled from semaphore to colour light over a 32-hour possession on 6th-8th August 1960. The station was completely rebuilt ahead of the start of electric services. From 5th September 1966 the CLC curve became a passenger route when Lime Street replaced Liverpool Central as the terminus for services from Manchester Central.

There followed another period of stability, this time lasting nearly 40 years. Allerton was chosen to be a new transport hub for South Liverpool and closed for a major rebuild from 31st July 2005 until 11th June 2006, when it reopened as Liverpool South Parkway. The station was upgraded with a footbridge accessible by stairs and lifts, greatly improved shelters, a travel centre and refreshment facilities; Garston station on the Merseyrail Northern Line (ex-CLC) was relocated 11 chains east to share the new facilities and name; and bus links were improved, including a frequent shuttle to Liverpool John Lennon Airport. Consequently more trains than ever before were scheduled to call.

36. This northward view from the up fast line platform appears to date from the 1930s. The station was known officially as Allerton for Garston & Woolton until 6th May 1974 when the suffixes ceased to be used. The platform buildings present a uniform appearance, all dating from the reconstruction of the station in 1891. They were of timber with generous awnings and heated by coal fires. The decorative rockeries could also be enjoyed at Wavertree and Mossley Hill. The houses in the background line Woolton Road. (Stations UK)

37. We move south to see Allerton Junction signal box on 22nd August 1954 as Stanier 4MT 2-6-4T no. 42607 runs past on the up fast. This loco and its classmate no. 42606 were regular engines on the Lime Street – Ditton – Warrington – Manchester Oxford Road service for much of the 50s. The ex-LNW box was situated immediately north of the bridge carrying our route across the CLC main line, as evidenced by the bridge girders. Allerton Junction itself is behind the photographer. (J.A.Peden/K.Lane coll.)

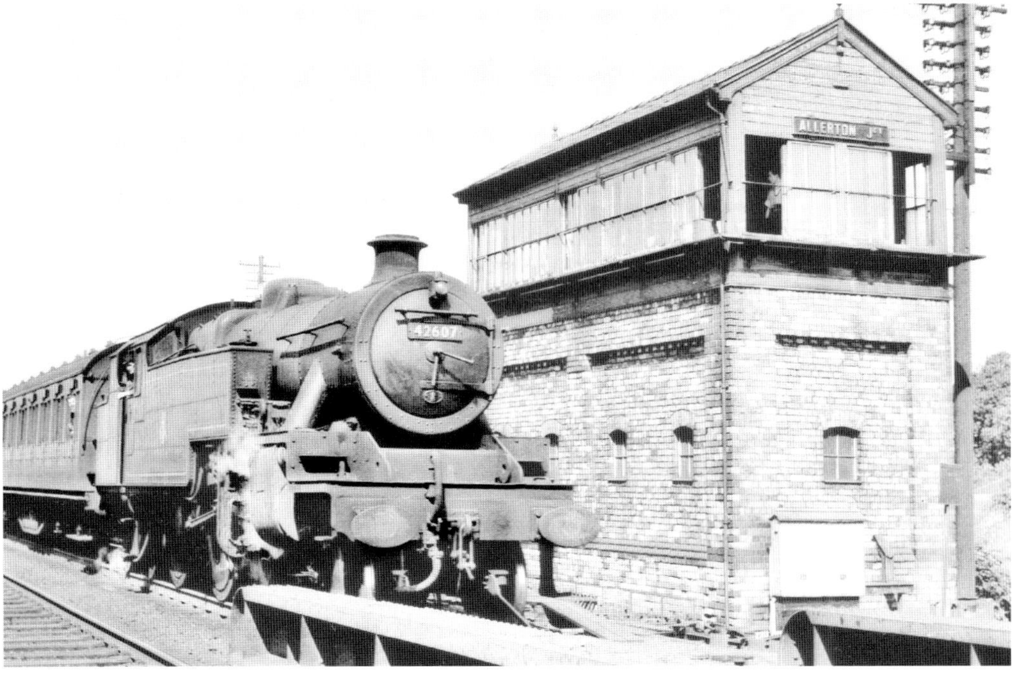

38. Now we have moved another 250 yards further south to a long footbridge that straddled the tracks just beyond Allerton Junction, which is in the left foreground. It's an early spring day in 1958 and Royal Scot 4-6-0 no. 46132 *The King's Regiment, Liverpool* is laying down a smokescreen as it runs along the up fast line with a class 5 goods. (The same engine was featured in picture no. 6, following which it was renamed in 1936, re-boilered in 1943, and had 40000 added to its number in 1948.) Halfway down the mixed consist we see the signal box, with the station behind the rear of the train. The sign to the right of the train is headed 'British Railways Modernisation' and tells passing travellers that near here will shortly be constructed the new TMD. Behind it is the CLC line with the carriage and wagon works beyond. (J.A.Peden/K.Lane coll.)

39. The CLC Curve was realigned a little to the south in 1959-60 to accommodate the new TMD, and we can see it branching off to left in this picture from 5th September 1966. Note the speed restriction for up trains onto the curve of 15mph, also the gleaming new running-in board. The perfectly lit train is a class 8 goods, Runcorn or Widnes - Edge Hill quite possibly since it appears to consist mostly of chemical wagons. Class 5MT 4-6-0 no. 45441 was allocated to Speke Junction and was withdrawn in the following February. We can see the down slow line is signalled for reversible working, and also the Garston Curve at right marked by the OLE. (T.Heavyside)

40. On 28th December 1983 we look north from the central island to platform 1 as EMU no. 304006 arrives with the 12.40 Lime St – Crewe. The 1961-built shelter has been vandalised, and the station looks generally unappealing. The class 304s were the mainstay of this service for over 30 years. They were initially painted in a dull green relieved by yellow lining, then in the 1970s they were painted in unlined Rail Blue. This two-tone livery of blue and off-white suited them best. They all lost one of their central trailers in the mid-1980s, ending their days as three-car sets. (A.C.Hartless)

LIVERPOOL SOUTH PARKWAY

41. The transformation from windswept suburban Allerton to the transport hub that is Liverpool South Parkway is evident from this view taken on 29th April 2014. The station has become a heavily engineered interchange served by regional services as well as local ones. As with all UK stations built in the 21st century, step-free access has been provided, and here we see the footbridge linking the four platforms with three lifts. The meagre shelters of the previous era have been replaced by generous canopies. At platform 1 DMU no. 156427 is calling with the 10.55 Lime Street – Manchester Oxford Road. (A.C.Hartless)

42. Also taken from the southern end of the island platform we see the edifice that stands on what was once the home of South Liverpool Football Club and which is a vast improvement on the street entrance on Woolton Road that served between 1961-2005. Far left is the modern-day entrance where passengers turn right to reach platforms 1-4 and go straight on along a covered walkway for Merseyrail platforms 5&6. All this cost a reported £32m, and required a period of closure six months longer than originally planned. But it soon became popular with the public, utilisation in 2019-20 was 2.663m. (A.C.Hartless)

43. On Grand National Day 14th April 2018 no. 57316 was on the rear of the departing 19.31 Northern Belle return excursion to London Euston with no. 57313 out of shot up front. On the left is Allerton Junction signal box. This replaced the LNW box from 8th August 1960 and served until 2nd January 2019 when its functions were transferred to Manchester ROC. The photographer is standing on platform 4, temporarily extended southward by 150m in order to accommodate Pendolinos on Euston services, which terminated here whilst Lime Street was closed for refurbishment. (D.Birmingham)

WEST OF SPEKE

Speke Junction

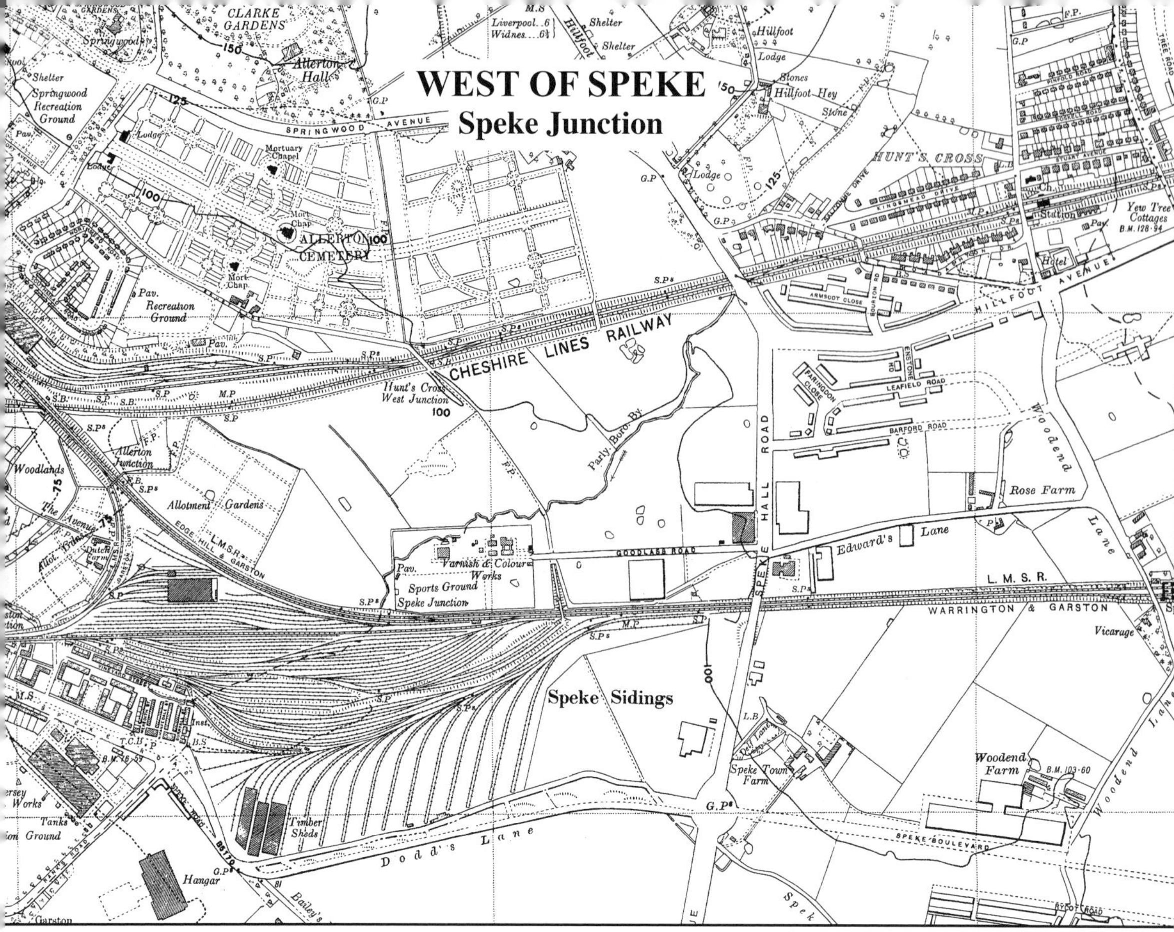

X. Speke Junction was created on 15th February 1864 when the LNW opened from Edge Hill to join the SHCR one mile west of Speke station. On 1st January 1873 the LNW completed a triangle with the Garston Curve as noted above. Within the triangle the LNW built Speke Junction locoshed, which was linked to the Garston Curve. On either side of the south side of the triangle Speke Sidings were constructed. This 1938 extract is derived from a 6ins to 1 mile map.

44. Speke Junction locoshed opened on 10th May 1886. It had 12 dead end straight roads designed to hold 60 locos, predominantly freight. In this eastward picture from around 1931 the building far left is the coal stage and the general impression is one of tidiness, not always the case in later years. It was coded 35 by the LNW, becoming 8C under the LMS, which it remained until closure on 6th May 1968. (J.Alsop coll./*Disused-stations.org.uk*)

45. Turning around on the footbridge used for picture 38 we see 9F 2-10-0 no. 92080 with a class 5 freight running along the down slow from the direction of Speke Junction towards Edge Hill. The date is probably April 1956 when the loco was brand new from Crewe; it appears to be running-in before going to its first allocation at Toton. At far left we can see new factories under construction near Speke Junction, and to the right is the locoshed. Above the train can be seen the mechanical coaling plant whilst the taller tower in front of the shed is the ash disposal plant; both of these were installed in 1955. (*Rail-online.co.uk*)

46. This is Speke Junction c1956 with Patriot 4-6-0 no. 45515 *Caernarvon* running past on the down main with a nine-coach express, the first three vehicles of which are GWR stock. On the left are factories constructed since WWII; Goodlass Wall was selling paint in Liverpool in the 1840s and, in 2022, was still trading from this site. Speke station was formerly beyond the second bridge in the background. Speke Junction signal box was the fifth version at this location, the other four having been progressively outgrown; it served from 1909-2018 and originally had 100 levers. The Garston Dock line runs behind the box, and the wagons just visible on the high-level line to its right occupy a small part of Speke Timber Yard, the eastern end of which later became Garston Car Terminal (GCT). (R.Humm coll.)

47. The rear of Speke Junction signal box dwarfs no. 86030 as it comes off the through siding on 1st April 1986 with the 12.34 to Dagenham carrying Ford Escorts manufactured at Halewood. Note Speke Down Sidings on the left and Garston Gas Works in the background. (P.D.Shannon)

48. 58-year-old no. 37716 of Direct Rail Services was yard pilot at GCT on 21st June 2021 and is shunting empty automotive flats. There are four sidings here each ending with a loading ramp. Most of the vehicles in the background are Ford Transit vans built in Turkey and railed here from Dagenham Dock for onward distribution. The main line is right, looking west towards Speke Junction. (D.Birmingham)

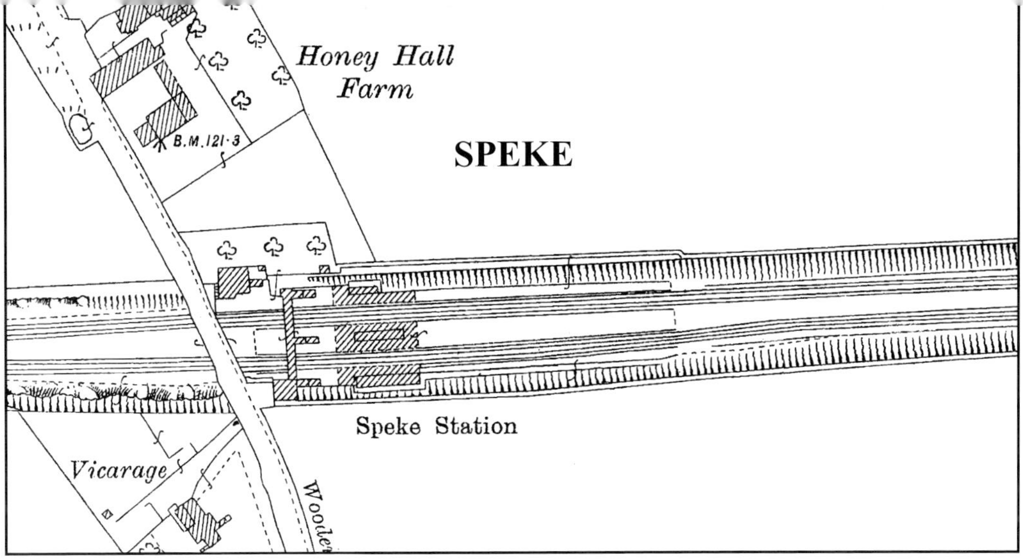

XI. Speke opened with the SHCR route on 1st July 1852 and was 1¾ miles from Allerton. There were no goods facilities. The station is believed to have had initially two side platforms but no photographs are known. It stood in open country ¾ mile north of the then small village of Speke and 1½ miles from medieval Speke Hall. Quadrupling of Speke Junction – Ditton Junction was implemented by the LNW in 1884 and the station was completely rebuilt with four platforms. However it was never well patronised and the LMS closed it from 22nd September 1930, ironically the year when passengers were first carried from nearby Liverpool (Speke) Airport. Speke village has grown into a large suburb but the station has never reopened, partly because Hunts Cross is only ½ mile to the north. This map is dated 1925.

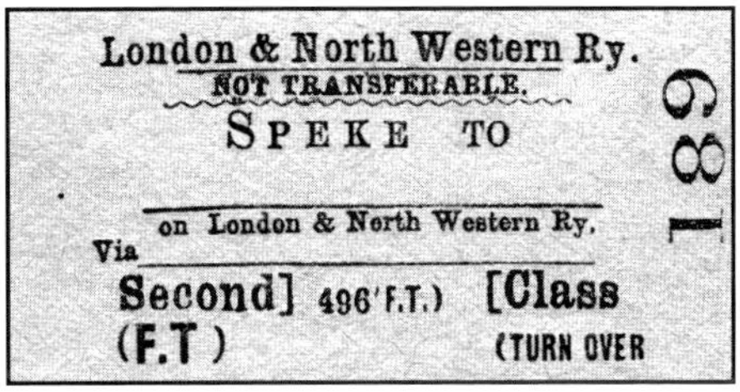

49. This south-west facing view is from around 1900 and shows the well-appointed station to have been tidily kept. An LNW 2-4-0 stands at the up slow platform. The street level entrance/exit was the southern one of a pair, the larger northern one is off camera to the right.
(Stations UK)

WEST OF HALEBANK
Woodside Siding / Halewood

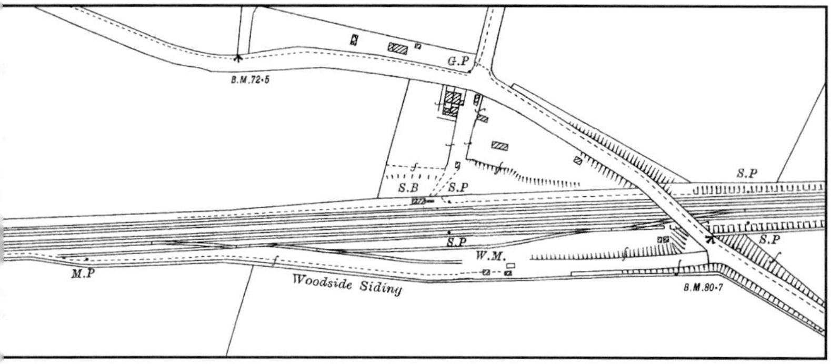

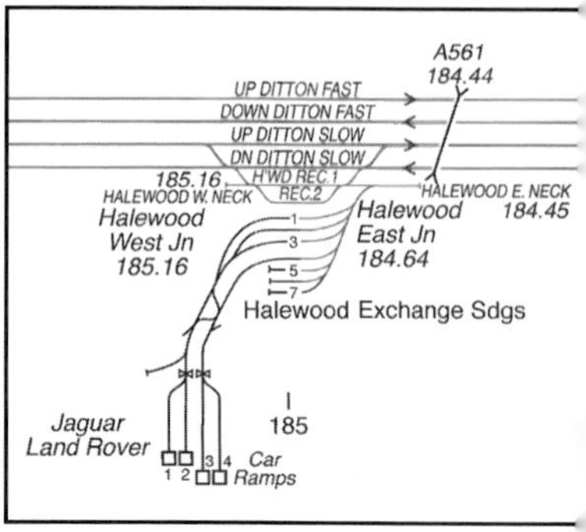

XIIa. This map extract is dated 1925.

XIIb. Track diagram dated 2018. (©TRACKmaps)

↓ 50. Goods traffic for Speke and Halebank was handled at Woodside Siding, set in open country 1½ miles east of Speke. This consisted of three sidings on the down side with a crane and weighing machine but no building. It handled only domestic coal after 20th April 1953 and closed entirely from 6th March 1961. On 2nd March 1959 5MT 4-6-0 no. 44768 passes the signal box (July 1884-11th December 1960) with an up express. The photographer is standing between the slow lines. Far left we see the two loop sidings trailing into the down slow. (K.Lane coll.)

↓*(bottom)* 51. In 1960 the Ford Motor Co. decided to build a new factory at Halewood, using a substantial greenfield site to the south and west of Woodside (beyond the bridge in the previous picture, on the left-hand side). This was rail connected from the down slow line. The factory commenced volume production of the Ford Anglia in October 1963. In 2001 Halewood began to build Jaguars, then owned by Ford, and from 2007 also Land Rovers. Tata Group bought the Jaguar Land Rover business in 2008, meanwhile Ford continued to make vehicle transmissions at the site. On 23rd April 2001 no. 66092 is seen reversing a long train of empty cargo wagons into the Jaguar plant. We are looking south-east with the exchange sidings behind the camera. (P.D.Shannon)

52. This is much the same position as picture no. 50 but taken from the trackside. On 23rd February 2015 no. 66084 has drawn its train of export Range Rovers out of the factory onto the ¼ mile long east neck siding, the eastern end of which was originally part of Woodside Siding. When the end of the train has cleared the exchange sidings it will reverse onto the west neck and then proceed across Halewood East Junction onto the up slow en route to Southampton Docks. (D.Birmingham)

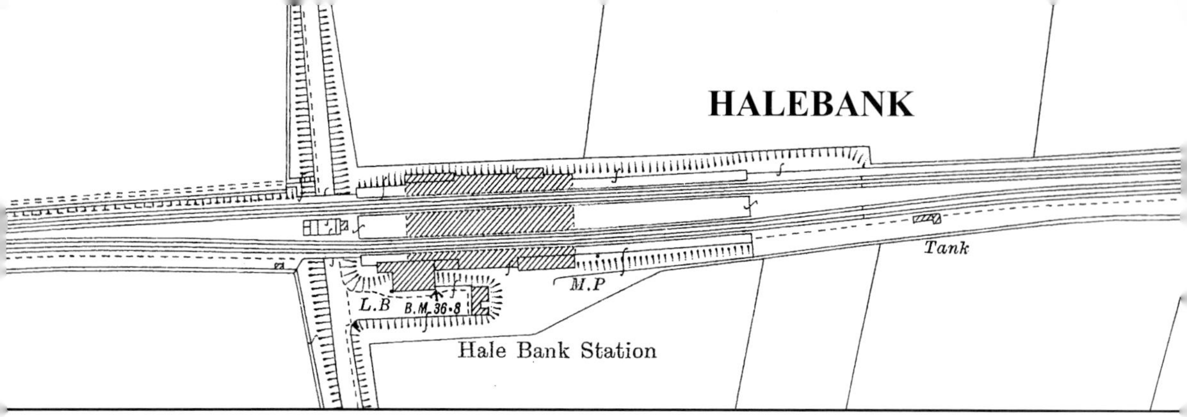

XIII. This opened with or soon after the SHCR's Garston Branch and was 2¼ miles from Speke. It was initially called Halewood Road and was a two-platform wayside station. It was renamed Halebank (for Hale) on 1st November 1874 to avoid confusion with the CLC's Halewood station, which had opened six months earlier and was 1¼ miles north-west. The locality is generally known as Hale Bank but the railway preferred the single word form. When Speke Junction – Ditton Junction was quadrupled Halebank gained two further platforms but surrounded as it was by farmland it was never well patronised. It closed temporarily between 1st January 1917 and 5th May 1919, and permanently from 15th September 1958. It was soon demolished as part of the modernisation of the line, leaving only the former station master's house, at ground level. This map is dated 1925.

↓ 53. The caption to this picture indicates it was taken post-closure. However, the station's appearance, with the buildings shorn of canopies, was the same in its last years pre-closure. The train is a Euston – Lime Street express hauled by rebuilt Patriot 4-6-0 no. 45527 *Southport*, an Edge Hill resident throughout the 1950s. The loco is just crossing the bridge over the subway which linked the platforms. The booking office, with four chimneys, is on the right, partially concealed by one of the two structures on the down slow platform. We can just see the further building is of standard timber construction similar to those at Allerton; the design was also present on the central island platform, but obscured by the train, and on the up fast, of which we see only the chimney. (P.H.Hanson)

↓*(bottom)* 54. The route between Speke and Ditton is gently undulating, and in the 1870s the LNW took advantage of a level section just east of Halebank to install water troughs. These were invented by John Ramsbottom, Locomotive Superintendent of the LNW, and first used on the North Wales main line in 1860. On 1st November 1958 8P 4-6-2 no. 46244 *King George VI* replenishes its tender whilst working the 12.18 SO Crewe – Lime Street. This is super power for such a light load; the loco had just left Crewe Works after a heavy intermediate overhaul and was running in before returning to its home shed of Carlisle Upperby, newly painted in maroon livery in place of Brunswick green. The distant building in the right background is Ditton Junction station.
(R.A.Whitfield/Rail Photoprints)

DITTON

XIV. The first station, called Ditton, opened as a temporary terminus of the SHCR's Garston branch on 21st May 1851 and became a through station on 1st July 1852. It was a simple affair of two side platforms set in open countryside. It closed on 1st May 1871 when Ditton Junction station opened 250 yards to the west, one mile from Halebank. Hale Road level crossing was converted to a bridge at this time.

Ditton Junction was quite a grand establishment, as shown on this 1938 extract (derived from a 6ins to 1 mile map). It was designed as an interchange between the SHCR and the LNW main line from Runcorn, which had opened to goods on 1st February 1869 and to passengers two months later. Initially there appear to have been two island platforms, with a third added when the line from Speke Junction was quadrupled. This was certainly the layout throughout the 1890s-1950s.

The St Helens service, locally known as 'The Ditton Dodger', was withdrawn on 18th June 1951. The station was completely rebuilt in 1960-61 as part of the Crewe – Liverpool electrification, but the Widnes – Warrington – Manchester trains were withdrawn from 10th September 1962 and the station's raison d'être ceased. It was renamed simply Ditton on 9th May 1973. The Chester service ended in 1975 and calls by trains on the Crewe – Liverpool route dwindled. Closure took effect from 29th May 1994.

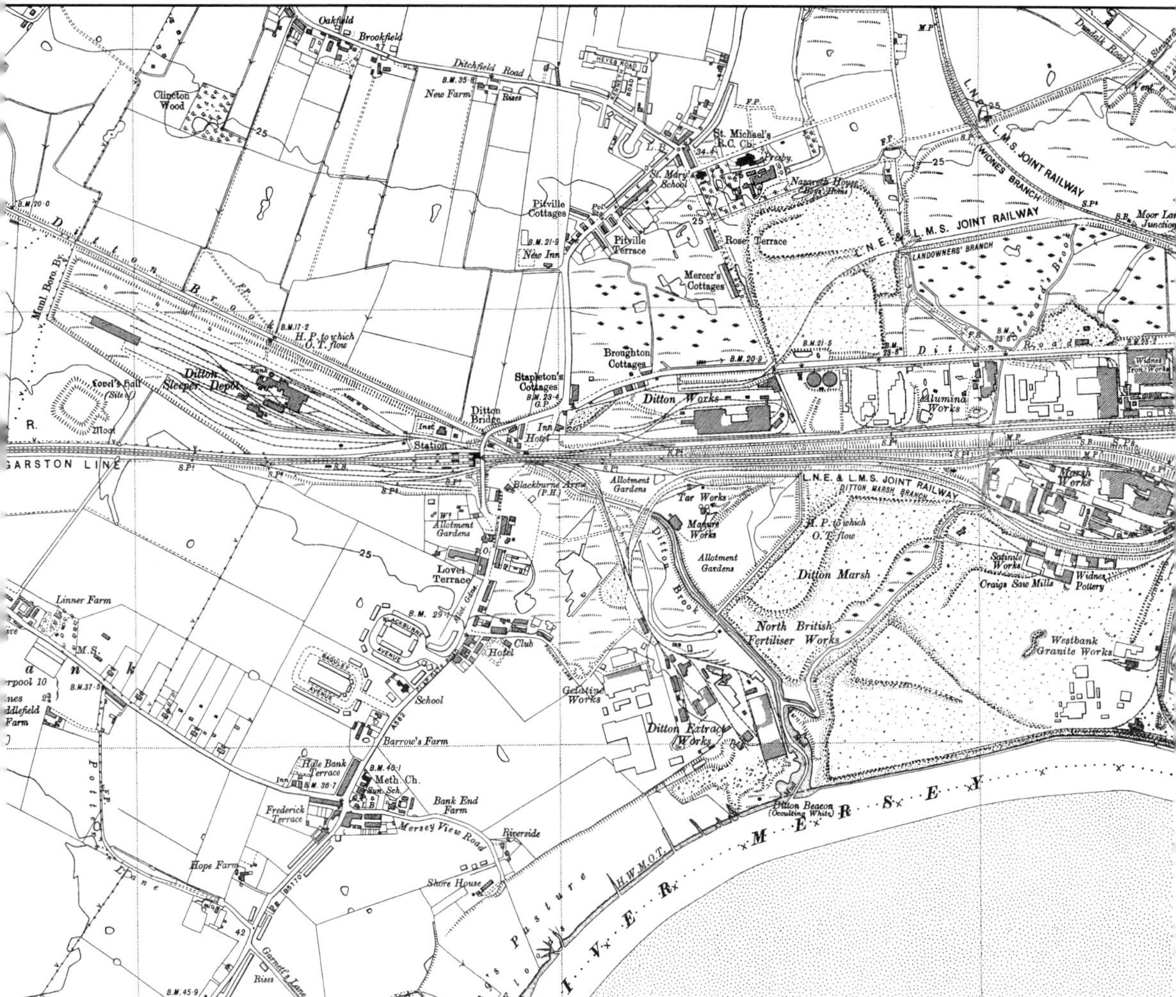

55. This is an eastward view from 1912. Ditton Junction No. 1 signal box at left served from 1884 until 22nd July 1956 when it was replaced by a new box on the opposite side of the lines. The signals behind the train, from left to right, controlled the original SHCR line from Widnes; the triple bracket was for the Runcorn line, and the other for the 1885 Widnes route. A passenger service is approaching from the Runcorn direction and is signalled straight ahead onto the down fast line. The picture was taken to illustrate the trackwork here following the derailment on 17th September 1912 of the 3.55pm Bangor – Lime Street summer only service. The train was signalled to cross to the down slow line, but the driver apparently misread the signals and was travelling at c60mph instead of the maximum permitted 15mph on the crossover. The entire train came off the rails and crashed into Hale Road bridge; fire broke out immediately. The death toll was 15 including the driver and fireman. This was the worst accident in the history of the Liverpool – Runcorn route. (8D Association)

56. This north-easterly view was taken in the early 1950s from the top of a water softening plant. In the centre of the picture is the rear of the booking office facing Hale Road, which crosses the line on a long bridge. From the rear of the building a covered footbridge gives access to three covered staircases down to the island platforms. The nearest island was the last built, spoiling the symmetry of the original design. The platform faces were numbered 1-6 coming towards the camera. Platform 1 was the up loop. Platforms 2 & 3 were the up and down fast lines, respectively. Platforms 4 & 5 were the up and down slow lines, and no. 6 was the down loop. The church tower in the distance was St Michaels at Nazareth House Boys Home. In 2022 the only structures remaining out of these were the derelict platforms. (H.Garnett/*Disused-stations.org.uk*)

57. This west facing view is from the late LMS or early BR period. It shows the ornate brickwork of the booking office frontage, and its lantern roof. Through the left hand arch we see the relief goods lines that gave access to the small goods yard; there was no building, but the map shows cattle pens. Goods closure was from 31st May 1965. Through the next arch we see platform 5 and an up goods at platform 4. The opening below the booking office reveals platforms 3 & 2. Next comes a water tower before the final arch through which some of the yard and sheds of the sleeper works are visible. This moved to Ditton from Garston c1910 and was in production until c2000. In the foreground we see some of the complicated trackwork between the east end of the station and the divergence of the Runcorn and Widnes routes. (Halton Borough Council/*Disused-stations.org.uk*)

58. Here we catch our first glimpse of a Ditton Dodger, departing platform 1 for St Helens in 1947. The loco is LMS no. 6676, one of a class of 160 Webb 1P 2-4-2Ts built by the LNW in the 1890s for light passenger work. 43 passed to British Railways in 1948; this one lasted until the end of 1949 and the last one was withdrawn in 1955. (W.A.Camwell/Stephenson Loco Soc.)

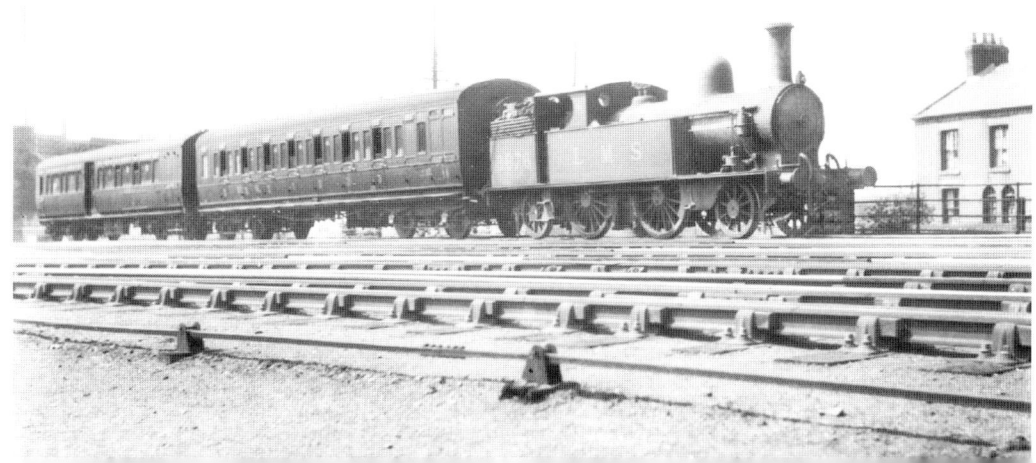

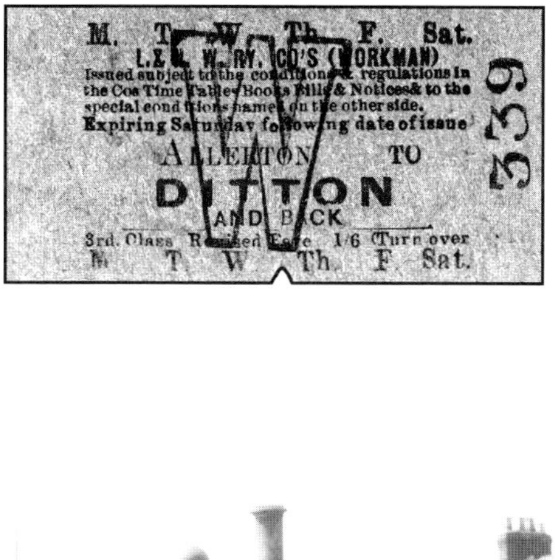

59. Platform 1 was generally used by passenger train departures towards Widnes. On Saturday 1st September 1962 2MT 2-6-2T no. 41211, shedded at Warrington Arpley, had propelled the three coach 4.19pm from Manchester Oxford Road, and the service terminated at platform 3. It then drew beyond the station to cross over to platform 1 to return in forward mode. The service was withdrawn after the following Saturday's trains. In the previous three years the station had been totally transformed with new prefabricated platform shelters, overhead electrification, and colour light signalling. However, it will be noted the down loop was not electrified; it was lifted c1970. The single track in the background led to the sleeper works. Note the shunt signal controlling the exit and the water tower for locos setting off on a long shift. (*Colour-Rail.com*)

60. On 7th July 1983 we see no. 25051 running up through platform 4 with an infrastructure train. The fence at left separates platform 5 from the abandoned platform 6, which was excluded from the station rebuild. Behind the train is Ditton Junction No. 2 signal box. This was a mechanical installation that replaced an earlier LNW box on 7th November 1960. It was in turn replaced by Ditton PSB on 9th December 2000. This was situated behind the reception sidings off camera to the left, and was replaced by a workstation at Manchester ROC in 2018. The sheds in the right background are the sleeper works. The station looks neglected and the station name on the lamp cover at right reads Ditto Junction. (P.D.Shannon)

61. This is the same view as in picture no. 55, 76 years later and compromised by OLE. On 24th February 1988 no. 58020 is heading empty coal hoppers from Garston Dock, most likely to one of the East Midlands collieries. To its right is Ditton Junction No.1 signal box, which served until the opening of the PSB. The single line looping around the box is the siding which at this time served the British Oxygen Co (BOC) plant, some of whose storage tanks can be seen above the box. Fiddlers Ferry Power Station, five miles distant, overlooks the view. (T.Heavyside)

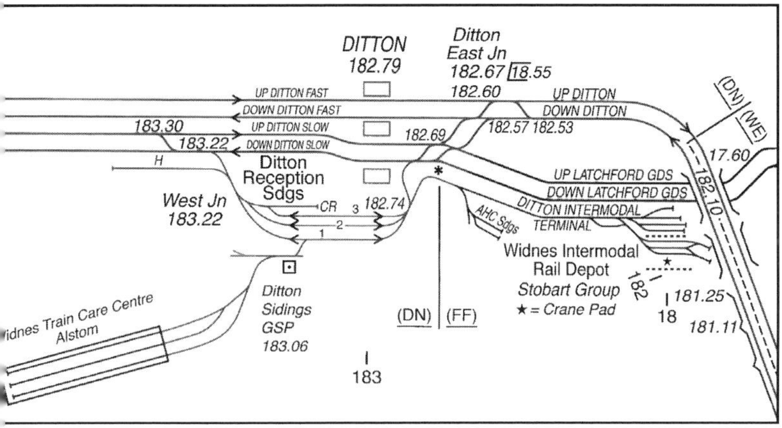

XIVa. Track diagram dated 2018. (©TRACKmaps)

↙ 62. Friday 27th May 1994 witnessed the last stopping trains before the station's closure. The final down service was the 17.30 Crewe – Liverpool, worked by DMU no. 142054 in Merseyrail yellow & white livery. During the brief stop a mock funeral procession took place. The last train of all was an hour later, the 18.41 Liverpool – Crewe, which was probably worked by the same train set. The photographer is positioned on platform 2. Top left of the picture we see one corner of the angular concrete, glass and timber booking office of 1960.
(M.Barber/
Disused-stations.org.uk)

63. The Marsh Works was one of the sites developed locally in the 19th century for manufacturing chemicals, particularly alkali derivatives, and became part of the Gaskell-Deacon works of Imperial Chemical Industries (ICI). After that closed, BOC was established between the late 1960s and mid-1990s. The site was again cleared and recycled as the Widnes Intermodal Rail Depot by the O'Connor Group, a local family concern, and subsequently acquired by the Stobart Group. On 12th July 1999 no. 47370 was photographed leaving the terminal with a well-loaded trip for Garston Freightliner Terminal (FLT). In the background the Ditton Junction – Runcorn line climbs towards Runcorn Bridge, off camera to the right, and we see the first half dozen arches of Ditton Viaduct. (P.D.Shannon)

64. The most exciting development in the railways of Widnes in this century has surely been the opening by Alstom, on 29th June 2017, of the Widnes Train Care Centre. This is located just west of Ditton, on the south side of the line. It is a three-track building, capable of accommodating an 11-coach class 390 Pendolino alongside shorter trains. The 13,000sqm facility is capable of building new trains and has a strong Research & Development and engineering presence. One of the first trains to pass through the centre was no. 390104, seen on opening day carrying the legend 'Longsight 175 years' and refreshed Virgin livery. When the Virgin franchise ended on 31st December 2019 the Pendolino fleet, designed by Alstom, passed to Avanti West Coast. (P.Wright)

NORTH OF RUNCORN
Runcorn Bridge

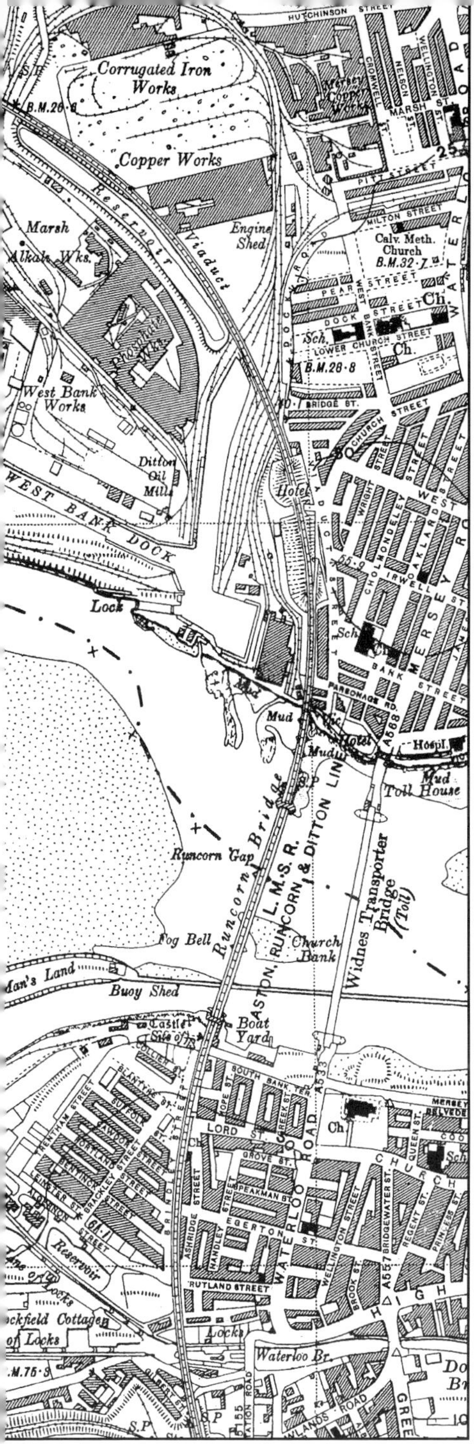

XV. This iconic bridge was designed by William Baker and constructed between 1863-68 to create a shorter rail route between Liverpool and the south which required a crossing of the Mersey Estuary. Runcorn Gap, where there had long been a ferry, was chosen as the location. The Admiralty stipulated there must be 75ft of clearance at high tide beneath the structure. This required an incline of 1:114 for around 1½ miles from Ditton Junction to the bridge.

The twin tracks climb from Ditton East Junction before curving southward and bridging the Widnes line (map XIV, near picture 54). The route then crosses the 49 span 792 yards Ditton Viaduct that bisects Widnes West Bank. It continues along a short embankment before reaching Runcorn Bridge, which comprises 16 brick arches, the three central lattice girder spans each of 305ft, and a further 33 brick arches on an upward gradient of 1:145 leading to Runcorn station; it is altogether 1,254 yards long. The final six arches of the northern approach and the three main spans cross the Mersey; the most southerly of the main spans also crosses the Manchester Ship Canal, opened in 1894. The southern approach viaduct crosses its predecessor, the Bridgewater Canal. This 1938 extract is derived from a 6ins to 1 mile map.

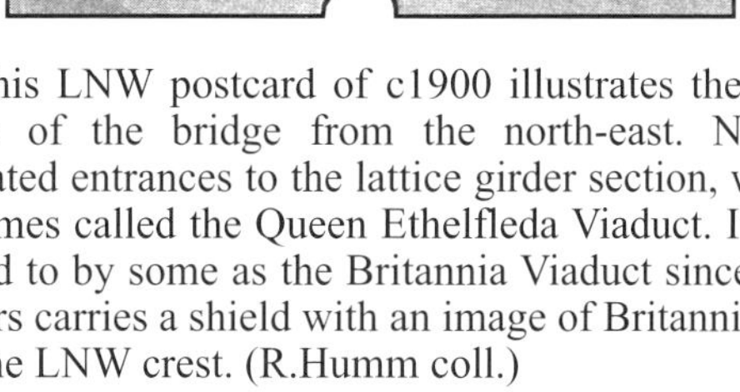

65. This LNW postcard of c1900 illustrates the central section of the bridge from the north-east. Note the castellated entrances to the lattice girder section, which is sometimes called the Queen Ethelfleda Viaduct. It is also referred to by some as the Britannia Viaduct since one of the piers carries a shield with an image of Britannia, taken from the LNW crest. (R.Humm coll.)

THE DEVONSHIRE
GREENALLS

↖ 66. In 1905 the UK's first transporter bridge opened between Runcorn and Widnes, a short distance upstream of the railway bridge. This served until 21st July 1961 when a fixed crossing in the form of a 527-yard steel through-arch bridge opened to road traffic between the rail and transporter bridges; in 1976 this became known as the Silver Jubilee Bridge. This picture, estimated from the summer of 1960, captures the Transporter Bridge on the far right and its incomplete replacement. The railway too is in transition; a Stanier 6P5F 2-6-0 hauls a southbound class 5 freight under recently installed OLE. Note the footpath adjacent to the railway; this crossed the central portion of the bridge and was open to the public for a small charge until 1965 when the right of way was diverted to the new road bridge. See also the dividing wall between the Mersey and the Ship Canal. (Catalyst Museum)

↑ 68. This picture shows the upper 14 arches of the northern approach on 26th June 1995 as no. 47742 comes off the central spans with Crewe – Lime Street empty mailvans. The train is quite dwarfed by the scale of the bridge. (D.Birmingham)

← 67. Here we see the southern approach on 27th August 1993 as no. 37706 leaves Runcorn station behind at far left with the 03.05 Lindsey refinery (Immingham) – Widnes fuel oil tanks. (P.D.Shannon)

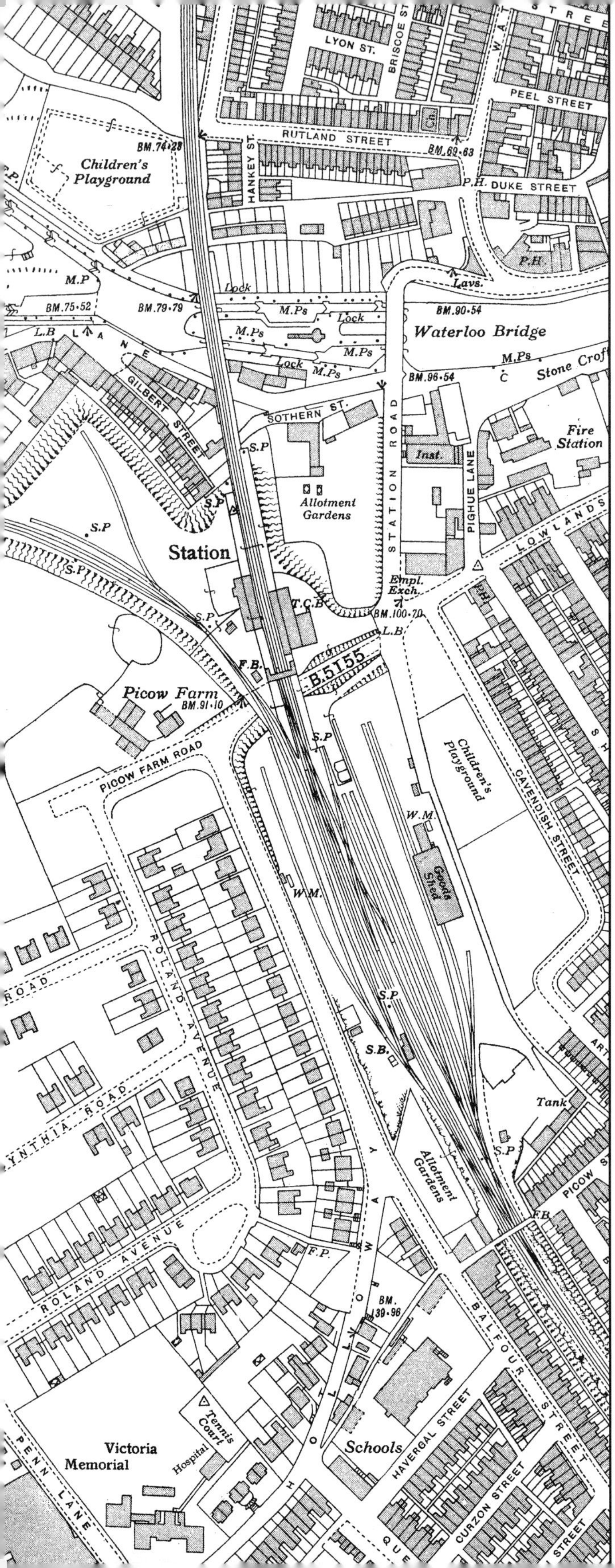

RUNCORN

XVI. Runcorn is believed to have been founded in 915AD by Queen Ethelfleda of Mercia as a fort to guard against Viking invasion up the Mersey Estuary. It remained a small, isolated settlement until the opening of the Bridgewater Canal from Manchester in 1776 and the establishment of a port. This encouraged the growth of industries including shipbuilding, chemicals, tanning and engineering. Runcorn is 2½ miles from Ditton Junction. It has been traditionally the principal stop between Liverpool (a little over 13 miles away) and Crewe. Usage in 2019-20 was 607,000. This map is dated 1937.

➚ 69. An early 20th century postcard illustrates the station's exterior, which is neat but not over-large. The main building faces the town, and a down passenger service is departing onto the bridge. (P.Laming coll.)

➔ 70. This view from c1910 is captioned 'The Mid-Day Mail L'pool to London stops at Runcorn'. A significant amount of the mail would have originated in North America and Ireland. We note at extreme right the booking office seen in the previous image and see there is a second building separating it from the platform, doubtless housing waiting rooms, etc. The covered footbridge is the only access to the down platform at the far end of which is a water crane. A visitor at the end of the 1950s would have found the platforms had been re-paved and signage updated, but little else had changed. (Lens of Sutton coll.)

➔ 71. Another transition image, from 26th October 1962, as 8F 2-8-0 no. 48296 slogs past with an up freight. The station was completely rebuilt in 1961 ahead of the inauguration of electric services. We see the modest up side building, the new footbridge with added clearances, and just visible a corner of the down side building. The OLE at far left marks the course of the Folly Lane branch. (*Colour-Rail.com*)

48296
RUNCORN

72. Another image from the same era shows a two-car class 108 DMU departing with a Lime Street – Chester local. One of the more evident changes delivered by the station rebuild was the significant extension of both platforms to avoid the time-taking practice of 'drawing-up' by long express trains. The view was obtained from the signal box and overlooks the Folly Lane branch. The flat-roofed up side buildings are visible behind the train, the Runcorn bridges above it, and the goods station at right; this looks busy here, but closed to everything except domestic coal from 18th January 1965 and entirely from 27th November 1967.
(R.W.Mercer/8D Association)

73. This was the view from the down platform on 19th August 2019 as Pendolino no. 390152 arrived with the 12.07 Euston – Lime Street. From left to right we see the multi-storey car park on the site of the goods station, the up side building, and the third generation footbridge which opened on 4th September 1994 with three lifts to provide step-free access including a western entrance across the Folly Lane branch.
(A.C.Hartless)

Runcorn Dock Branch

➔ XVII. This extract, dated 1938, is derived from a 6ins to 1 mile map. The first dock, later the Old Dock, opened in 1791 and was linked to the Bridgewater Canal. Additional docks followed, including further south at Weston Point. The railway was a relatively late arrival in 1869 and stimulated extra wharfage, whilst the opening of the Manchester Ship Canal 25 years later was another major development. Two significant businesses developed here in the late 19th century: the Weston Point Salt Works, the UK's leading producer of vacuum salt, and the Castner-Kellner Alkali Works, which became a founding constituent of ICI in 1926. Until 1970 the latter included a power station which required six trainloads of coal a day. Both sites had internal rail systems linked to the Dock Branch, in the case of Castner-Kellner by the Weston Point Light Rly. In 2022 both these sites were part of Ineos Group Ltd, successor to ICI. *[continued right...]*

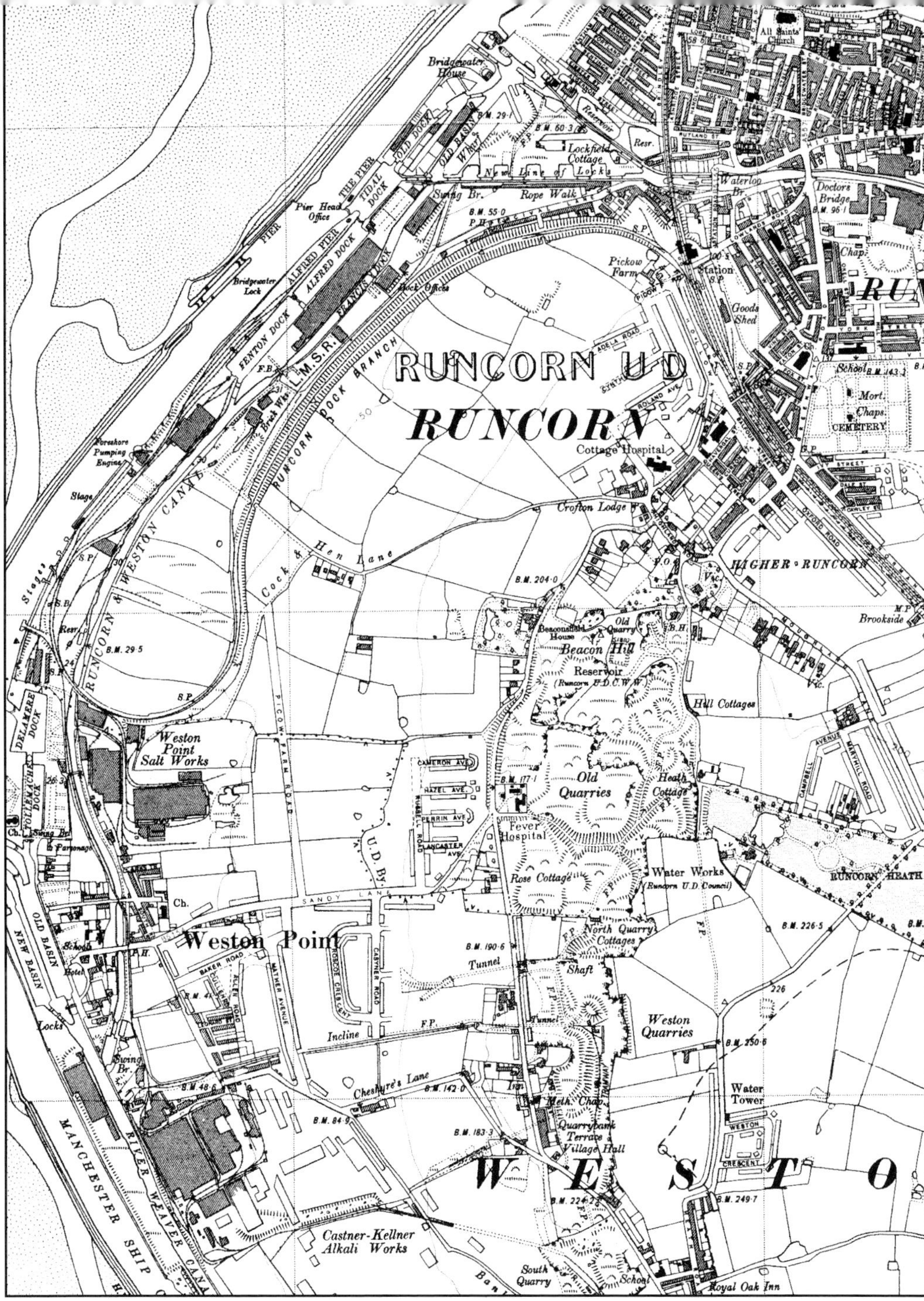

[continued from left] Runcorn Docks closed to wagonload rail traffic from 1st December 1950 and all rail traffic had ended by 1962. The branch now terminated at Folly Lane exchange sidings north of the salt works and was electrified at the same time as the main line. ICI traffic kept it open until March 1994, when the OLE was dismantled and the branch mothballed. It reopened from 28th March 2002 when rail traffic resumed from the salt works, and from 17th December 2013 activity was augmented by the opening by Viridor Energy of a power station fuelled by pelletised domestic waste, much of which is brought in by rail from Manchester.

74. Jim Peden was a railway historian and collector in addition to being a fine photographer. This splendid portrait of Peckett 0-4-0ST *Balfour*, works number 522 of 1891, and its crew was taken at Castner-Kellner c1910. (J.A.Peden coll./Industrial Railway Society)

& North Western Ry
indictable fraud and it must be given up on the
date of expiry otherwise no renewal will be
granted. RUNCORN BRIDGE
CONTRACT TICKET
BETWEEN
RUNCORN & WIDNES
Available for One Week including days
of issue and expiry
Fare -/9
6982

75. On 22nd January 1973 Yorkshire Engine 0-6-0DE no. 2718/58 *Eskdale* crosses Sandy Road level crossing on the Weston Point Light Railway with caustic soda tanks being tripped from Folly Lane to Castner-Kellner. ICI replaced its steam fleet here with diesels in 1960, but this particular one had recently arrived from its Billingham factory. (D.Pool/8D Association)

76. ICI retired its diesel fleet c1989 and BR took over responsibility for the remaining work. On 23rd November 1991 no. 31106 leaves Weston Point Salt Works with loaded wagons to Dalry. (P.D.Shannon)

77. On 23rd April 1993 we see no. 37713 leaving Folly Lane yard with the 13.45 empty fuel oil tanks to Stanlow refinery. There were 10 roads available at this time, of which the three furthest right were electrified. (P.D.Shannon)

78. On a late afternoon in June 2015 no. 66518 runs onto the Folly Lane line with a payload of domestic waste from Northenden, overlooked by Runcorn signal box. This replaced an LNW box in January 1940 and was designed as an Air Raid Precautions type to withstand bomb blast. It was de-commissioned on 4th May 2018 when its activities transferred to Manchester ROC, but in 2013 it was listed Grade II so has not been demolished. (D.Birmingham)

SOUTH OF RUNCORN

The line climbs from Runcorn at 1:101/115 to reach the watershed between the Mersey and Weaver valleys near Sutton Weaver. This was farming country until the growth of Runcorn New Town in the 1970s. At Halton Junction, $1\frac{1}{4}$ *miles from Runcorn, the* $1\frac{1}{2}$ *mile long Frodsham Branch, aka the Halton Curve, opened on 1st May 1873, joining the Warrington – Chester line and creating a through route from Lime Street to Chester and North Wales. It has had a chequered career as outlined under 'Passenger Services'. Frodsham Junction at the south end of the branch is illustrated in* Chester to Warrington.

During WWII a down goods loop was added to the main line south of Halton Junction and was known as Rocksavage after the Elizabethan mansion which stood close to the Frodsham Branch. The loop was removed in the 1950s.

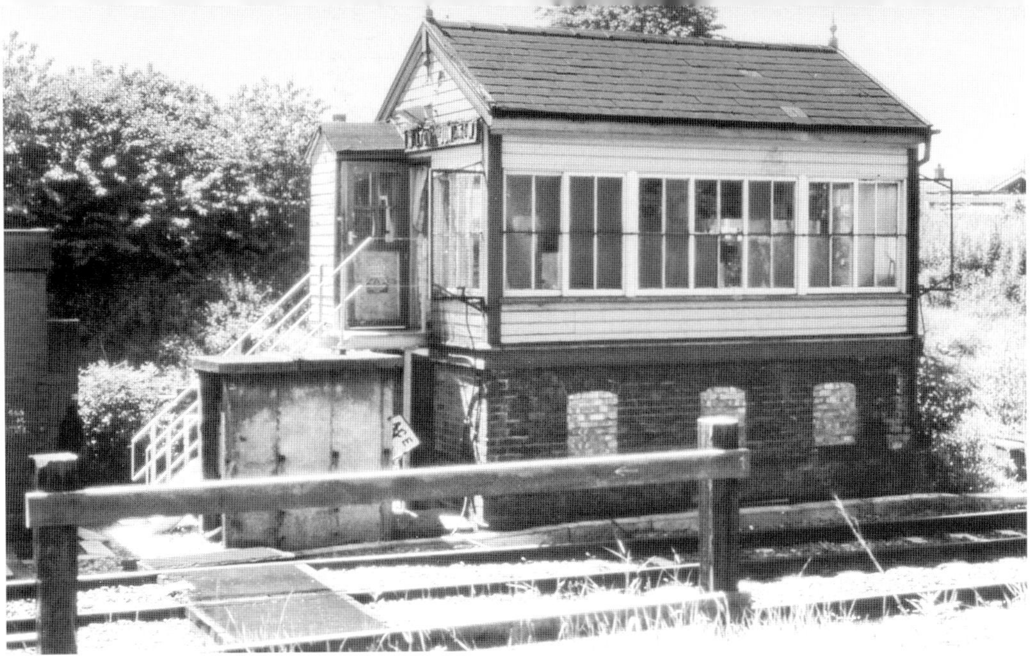

⬋ 79. South of the station the railway passed through Higher Runcorn, a prime residential area that developed in the late Victorian era. In July 1951 Britannia Pacific no. 70015 *Apollo* accelerates 'The Red Rose', 5.25pm from Lime Street to Euston, away from Runcorn. The loco was only a few weeks old and was allocated to Camden; the long train appears to consist almost entirely of BR mark 1 stock which was also brand new, making this the latest word in a modern express train, 'British Railways Standard'. (R.A.Whitfield/Rail Photoprints)

80. Halton Junction signal box was recorded on 29th May 1997. It was installed in the vee of the junction in July 1897, replacing an earlier nearby Saxby & Farmer box, and had 25 levers; it closed from 4th May 2018 after which it was demolished. (D.Birmingham)

81. Sometime in 1948 LMS 5XP 4-6-0 no. 6004, originally named *Princess Louise*, was recorded waiting for the road from Rocksavage goods loop. Built in 1920, it was the last surviving of the 130 Claughtons and was shedded at Edge Hill. It lasted until April 1949 when it was called to Crewe for the last time. (R.A.Whitfield/Rail Photoprints)

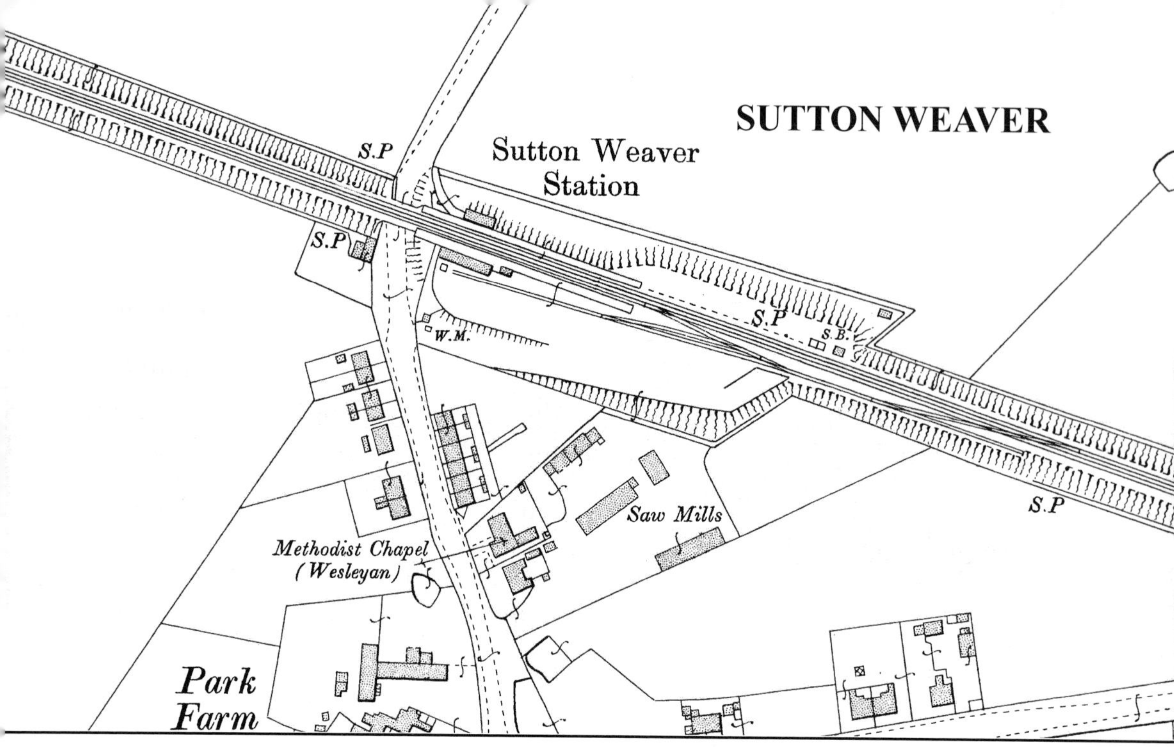

XVIII. Sutton Weaver was a little over three miles south-east of Runcorn. It served the village of Sutton; it would seem the LNW added the suffix to distinguish it from other Suttons and the expanded name was formally adopted by the village some years later. It opened with the line in 1869 and had a goods siding on the down side. The station closed to passengers from 30th November 1931 and to goods from 30th April 1942. (Halton station on the Chester – Warrington line was only ½ mile away but this too closed, in 1952.) Since the creation of Runcorn New Town the area north of the line has been heavily developed, and the M56 passes beneath, half a mile to the east. In 2022 the station site could still be identified by an emergency trailing crossover. This map is dated 1908.

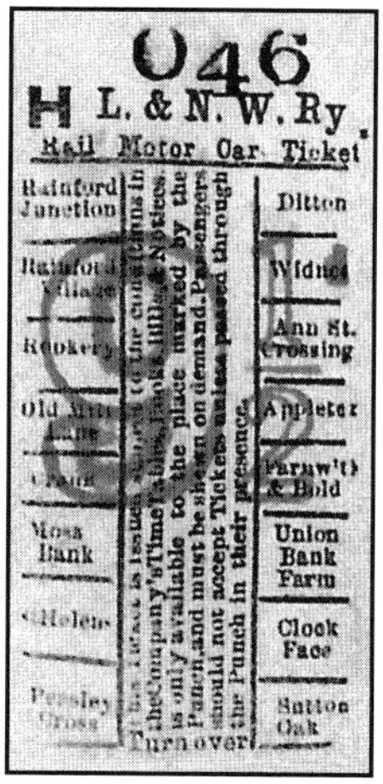

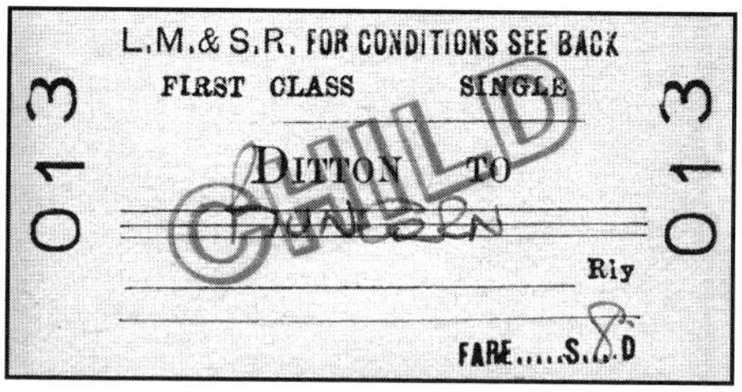

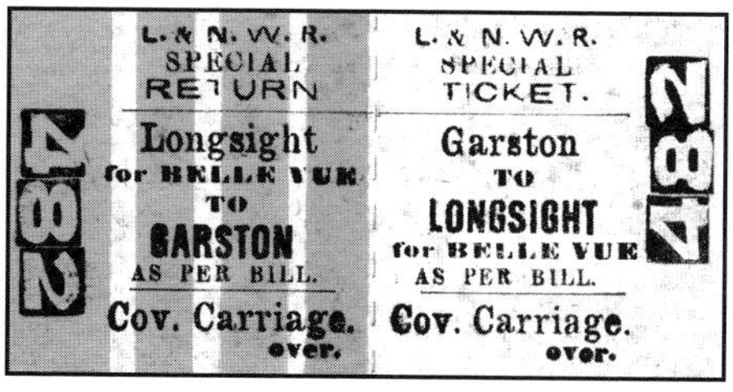

82. Seven folk are giving their attention to the photographer whilst a train approaches from the Liverpool direction circa 1905. The goods siding is visible far left. A quarter mile in the distance the line crosses the route of the Chester - Warrington line, which is in tunnel at that point. (*Railwaystationphotographs.com*)

83. In this 1949 shot, unrebuilt Royal Scot 6P 4-6-0 no. 46113 *Cameronian* crosses Sutton Fields Farm bridge on the approach to the station site with a Crewe – Lime Street local. The loco carries its BR number but still shows LMS on its tender. It was rebuilt with a Stanier boiler the following year and thereafter spent the rest of its BR career working in the West Riding, mostly from Leeds Holbeck. (R.A.Whitfield/Rail Photoprints)

***Our line joins the former Grand Junction route of 1837 at Weaver Junction, two miles beyond Sutton Weaver, to continue south to Crewe, as featured in* Crewe to Wigan.**

2. Speke Junction – Garston Dock

The 2½ miles between Speke and Garston were plain track when opened by the SHCR on 1st July 1852 except for sidings at the terminus.

EAST OF GARSTON CHURCH ROAD

Garston Junction

84. On 1st April 1986 we see no. 56066 bringing empty HAA coal wagons into Speke Up Sidings from Garston Dock before proceeding to Mansfield. Garston Junction signal box was in the vee between the lines from Speke Junction, left, and from Allerton East Junction, far right. It served from 1908-2002 when its duties were transferred to Speke Junction. The Garston Curve was singled from 2nd January 2019. The junction can be seen in map X, near picture 44, although the signal box is omitted. (P.D.Shannon)

GARSTON CHURCH ROAD

➚ XIX. The 1938 map, derived from a 6ins to 1 mile version, adjoins map X. The SHCR line enters on the right, adjacent to Speke Road, and crosses Church Road immediately before the station (marked 'Sta.'), which opened on 1st March 1881 in response to the development of nearby housing. Trams from Liverpool via Aigburth reached Garston c1900, running the length of St Mary's Road to a terminus close to the station in Speke Road where the Tramway Depot is marked. This no doubt impaired the level of train travel. The station was temporarily closed between 5th April 1917 and 5th May 1919, and permanently from 3rd July 1939. Its subsequent demise was piecemeal; as part of the electrification works in 1961 the down platform was removed and the down line re-aligned; also the up line was lifted. The up platform and building were demolished c1971 and the down line was closed on 15th August 1977. The route through the former station was subsequently utilised by the A561 Garston Way. However the tracks immediately to the south of the station remained in use serving Garston FLT.

➔ 85. This is an eastward view from 5th October 1906. The station buildings are of typical LNW pre-fabricated timber design. An 0-6-0PT can be seen shunting coal wagons beyond the station on the docks lines. The buildings to the right of the tracks are mostly those of Garston gas works. (Stations UK)

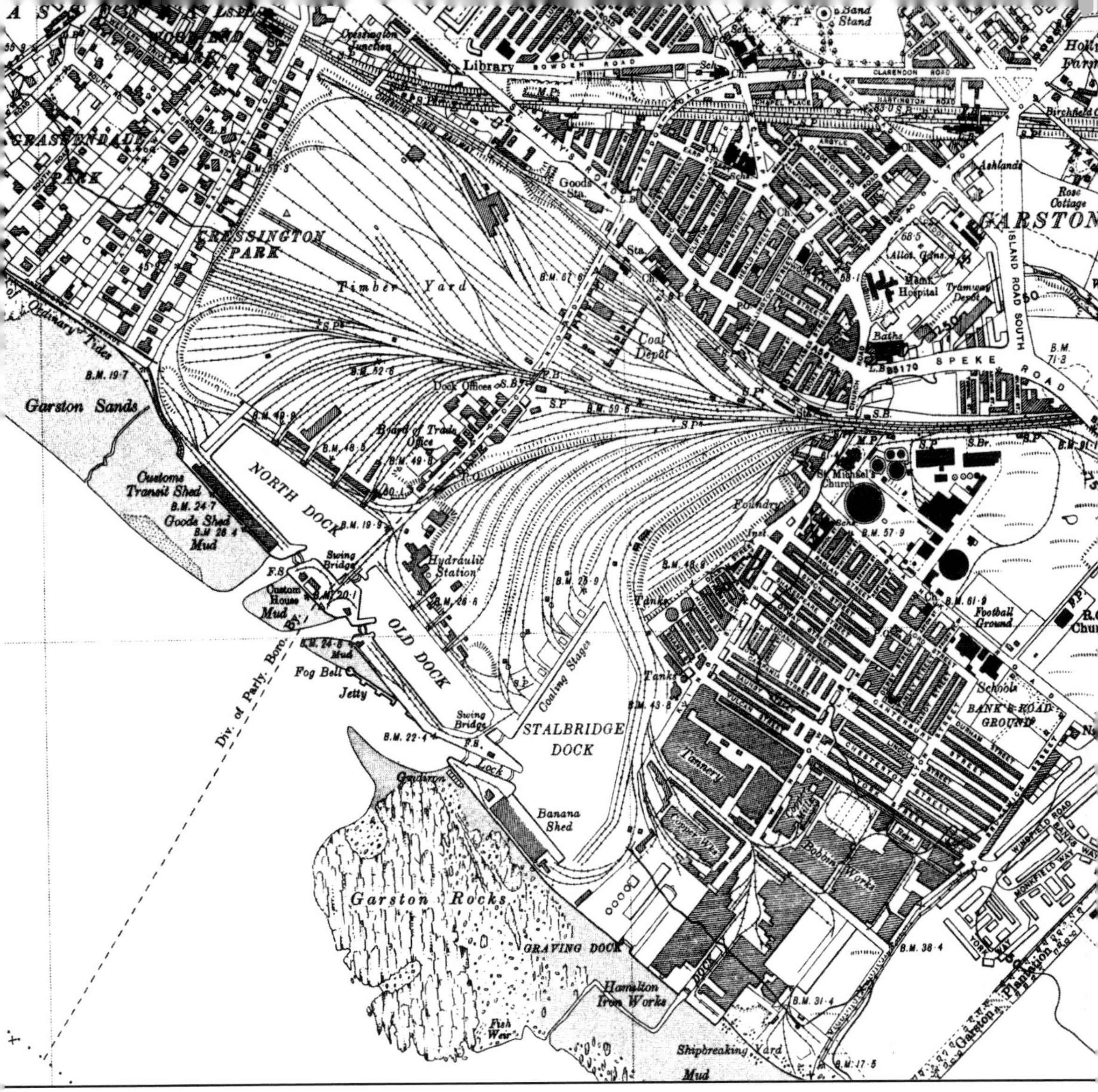
Library
Bowden Road
Clarendon Road
Band Stand
Garston
Grassendale Park
Cressington Park
Timber Yard
Goods Sta.
Coal Depot
Island Road South
Speke Road
Hospital
Tramway Depot
Baths
Ashlands
Rose Cottage
Garston Sands
Customs Transit Shed
Goods Shed
Mud
North Dock
Swing Bridge
Custom House
Old Dock
Fog Bell
Jetty
Dock Offices
Board of Trade Office
Hydraulic Station
Coaling Stages
Stalbridge Dock
Lock
Banana Shed
Gridiron
Garston Rocks
Graving Dock
Hamilton Iron Works
Fish Weir
Shipbreaking Yard
St. Michael's Church
Foundry
Football Ground
Schools
Bank Road Ground
Tannery
Bobbin Works
Div. of Parly. Boro.
Garston Plantation

86. Probably taken in 1970, this picture captures a line up of three container trains getting ready to leave the FLT. This was built c1965 on the former coal depot and near the site of the two-road SHCR loco shed, which was replaced by Speke Junction. From left to right we see: type 4 diesel no. 411, later 50011, displaying train code 4S55, destination Scotland, possibly Coatbridge; resident shunter no. 4135, later 08905; AL5 electric no. E3072, later 85017, on 4E79, destination most likely Felixstowe; and an AL6 electric showing 4O60 for Southampton. (Rail Online)

87. On 2nd April 1986 no. 58029 leaves the docks with empty HAA wagons destined for one of the Midlands collieries. Far left is the parapet of Church Road bridge, and a class 08 pilot can be seen in the middle distance. On the right is Garston (Church Rd) signal box. This was built in 1906 and replaced a box some 25 years older that stood at the station; it eventually closed on 13th June 1993. Church Road station was behind the train, beyond the road bridge. (P.D.Shannon)

GARSTON DOCK

The station can be seen on the map, also marked 'Sta.', immediately before the crossing with Dock Road. The first dock opened on 21st June 1853, and two further docks, North Dock and Stalbridge Dock, were later added to cope with demand. In the mid-1930s it was reckoned the docks had 70 miles of sidings. Coal exports ceased around 1996 and the last sidings closed, but in 2022 the port was still active, dealing with cargoes such as scrap metal, cement and other bulk commodities.

On 1st June 1864 an end-on junction west of Garston station was made with the Garston & Liverpool Railway, which ran to a temporary terminus at Brunswick, later extended to Liverpool Central. This small concern became a founder member of the CLC in 1866. The section of line from Garston (LNW) to Cressington Junction (top of map) closed to passengers from 2nd September 1873 following the opening of the CLC's own line from Cressington to Manchester, the first station on which was also named Garston (top right by Woolton Road bridge). To reduce confusion, the LNW station was renamed Garston Dock on 1st March 1881. As with Church Road it was temporarily closed during 1917-19, but unlike its neighbour it remained open during WWII only to succumb to final closure from 16th June 1947. The line from Church Road to Cressington Junction closed entirely from 15th August 1977 and the section through the station site was obliterated by the A561 Garston Way.

🡑 88. This 1922 west-facing view illustrates the platform structures. The larger canopy was on the arrivals (down) platform, beyond which a brick arch led to Dock Road that crossed the line on the level. At the end of the up platform is the booking office cum entrance partially obscured by a hut. Beyond the level crossing to the left of the tracks the LNW established a sleeper factory, which was transferred to Ditton Junction before WWI, following which the area was used as a storage yard for imported timber. (Stations UK)

🡐 89. This 1947 view was taken shortly before the end of the passenger service. LMS Coal Tank 2F 0-6-2T no. 7751 awaits departure with a modest but clean train set. The down platform appears to have become overgrown by this time, and the direction of the crossover has been altered since the earlier picture. (W.A.Camwell/ Stephenson Loco Soc.)

90. On Saturday 6th June 1959 the Stephenson Loco Society and the Manchester Loco Society jointly ran a railtour around a number of lines on Merseyside, which culminated in a run along the SHCR from St Helens Shaw Street to Garston Dock, where it reversed before the final leg to Lime Street. This was the last known train to call at Garston Dock. It arrived behind 7F 0-8-0 no. 49434 with classmate no. 49224 on the rear. The former then ran round the train, as illustrated, and the two locos double headed to Lime Street. (*Colour-Rail.com*)

91. Spot the 16-ton BR standard coal wagon! It is (apparently) above the bridge of the *SS Ballylesson*, tilted from one of Garston Port's coal staithes to discharge its load into the ship's hold. Ballylesson is a village in County Down, so it's a fair bet the ship is a collier bound for Belfast. This picture of a once commonplace activity was taken in August 1980. (R.Humm)

3. Ditton Junction – Warrington

WEST OF WIDNES SOUTH

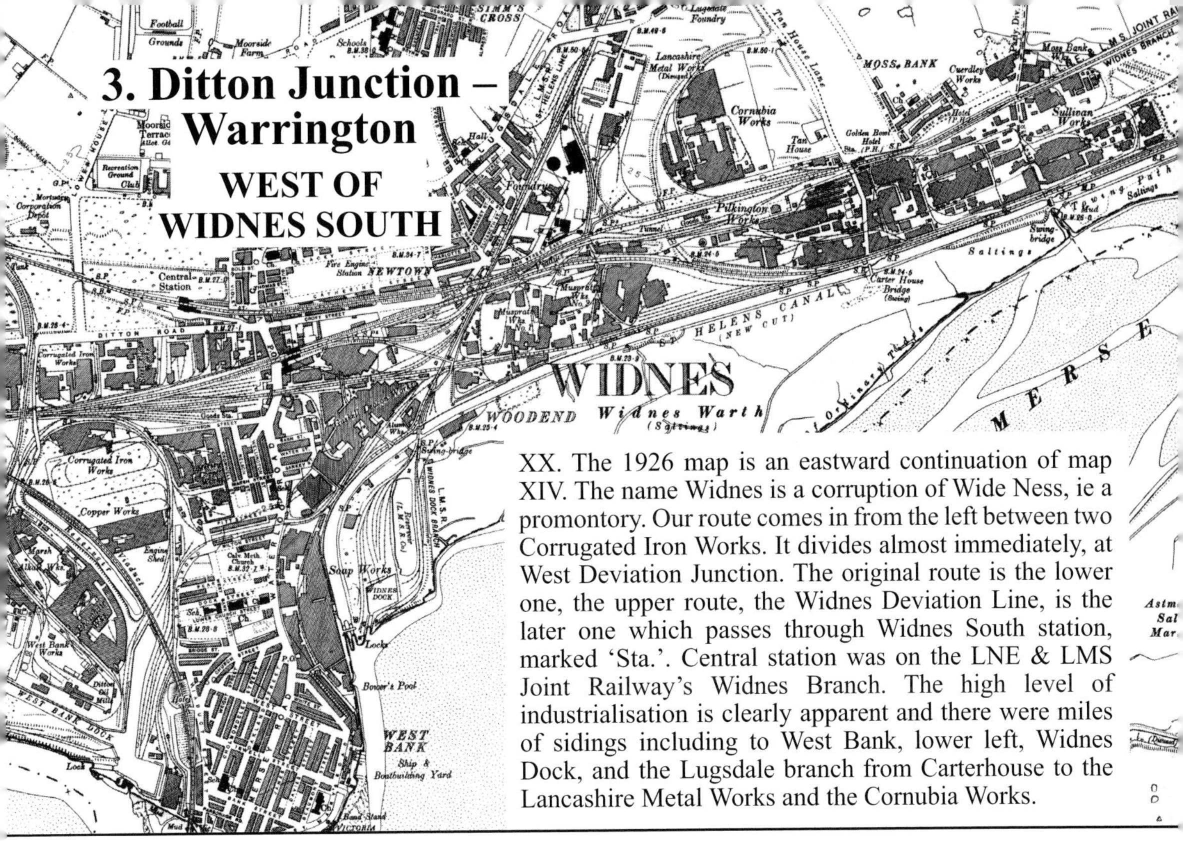

XX. The 1926 map is an eastward continuation of map XIV. The name Widnes is a corruption of Wide Ness, ie a promontory. Our route comes in from the left between two Corrugated Iron Works. It divides almost immediately, at West Deviation Junction. The original route is the lower one, the upper route, the Widnes Deviation Line, is the later one which passes through Widnes South station, marked 'Sta.'. Central station was on the LNE & LMS Joint Railway's Widnes Branch. The high level of industrialisation is clearly apparent and there were miles of sidings including to West Bank, lower left, Widnes Dock, and the Lugsdale branch from Carterhouse to the Lancashire Metal Works and the Cornubia Works.

92. The original alignment of the Garston line of the SHCR is the trackwork, abandoned in 1966, in the right of this image from 22nd February 1990. The train is a Gladstone Dock – Fidlers Ferry coal haul behind nos 20045 and 20159 and is running along the 1885 alignment from when Ditton Junction – West Deviation Junction was quadrupled. In the left background the Runcorn line climbs towards Ditton Viaduct, crossing the Widnes route. The abandoned abutment in the left foreground carried the LNE/LMS goods branch to Ditton Marsh. Just out of shot on the right was Widnes West Deviation signal box. This replaced an LNW box of 1874 on 12th February 1967 and was a flat-roofed structure of standard BR LMR design, which closed on 19th December 1988 following the demise of Hutchinson Street Goods. (P.D.Shannon)

93. Now we look the other way, 21 years earlier on 13th August 1968. On the left the Deviation climbs to pass through the site of Widnes South station, and Widnes No. 7 signal box is visible at the top of the incline. The line disappearing beneath the footbridge at far right is the original SHCR line towards Widnes Dock. The bridge is at Waterloo Road where the station was located from 1852-70 and Widnes No. 5 signal box stood until the year of this picture. In the centre of the picture is Hutchinson Street Goods Yard. A Drewry 0-6-0 shunter is yard pilot and an English Electric Type 4 is coupled to a rake of cartics. The two tracks in the right foreground led to West Dock. In 2022 the only lines surviving from this view were the Deviation route. (D.Pool/8D Association)

WIDNES SOUTH

One of the first acts of the LNW on taking over the SHCR was to rename Runcorn Gap station to Widnes from 1st September 1864, to avoid confusion with Runcorn itself. The station had relocated from Widnes Dock with the opening of the Garston branch on 1st July 1852; a contemporary map shows it in open countryside at what became Waterloo Crossing. The growth of industry thereafter was rapid and the LNW found the flat crossing at Widnes Dock Junction (pictures 109-111) a cause of such congestion that a bypass was needed. A new east-west line, the Widnes Deviation, was opened on 1st November 1869, a short distance north of the original route and at a higher level to avoid flat crossings with either railways or roads. The passenger station was relocated thereon on 1st March 1870 only around 100 yds from the previous site. It was 1¾ miles from Ditton Junction. British Railways renamed it Widnes South from 5th January 1959 only a short while before closure, which took effect from 10th September 1962. There were occasional special trains until around 1965.

➚*[top]* 94. A Ditton Dodger stands at the down platform before proceeding to Ditton in 1948. We see the driver in his cab and an LNW 2-4-2T providing the motive power at the rear of the train. This has arrived via the spur from Ann Street visible between Widnes No. 7 signal box and the huts just beyond it. The main line ran straight on. The junction closed from 18th April 1982 along with the signal box. (W.A.Camwell/Stephenson Loco Soc.)

➚*[middle]* 95. The structures at platform level did not change greatly during the station's life. This eastward view from 1957 records the symmetrical canopies backed by modest buildings heated by coal fires. BR 2MT 2-6-0 no. 78039 is at the end of the up platform waiting for a signal to proceed to the locoshed.
(H.C.Casserley/*Disused-stations.org.uk*)

➔ 96. The exterior is seen from the down platform after its renaming to Widnes South. This was to distinguish it from Widnes North on the former CLC route, itself renamed from Farnworth on 5th January 1959.
(R.Martindale/*Disused-stations.org.uk*)

WIDNES SOUTH STATION

Widnes Locoshed

The LNW built a three-road shed in 1874 and doubled its size in 1881 to accommodate 24 engines. It was coded 35W, sub-shed of Speke Junction. In 1935 the LMS re-coded it 8D, which it retained until closure from 13th April 1964. It was located on a confined site between the Deviation line and the Widnes South – Ann Street spur to which it connected.

97. This 6th January 1961 view, taken from the long footbridge leading to the harbour, captures a quiet moment at 8D. The two tracks nearest the camera are the Garston Curve of 1852. The two Stanier 3MT 2-6-2Ts nos 40134/43 were stored out of use here for over 12 months and were eventually withdrawn in the following October. Descending behind them is the Widnes South – Ann Street line. Then comes the six-road shed. Above the unidentifiable 8F can be seen the Deviation line whilst behind the 2MT 2-6-2T is the coaling stage. The turntable was off shot to its right. (E.Bellass/8D Association)

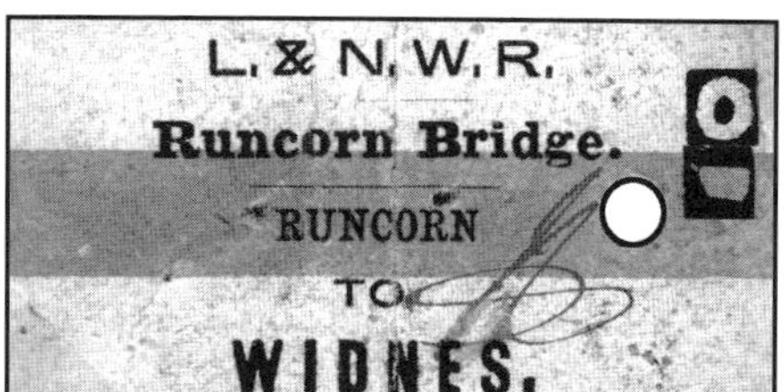

EAST OF WIDNES SOUTH

98. The Deviation was 1¼ miles long and rejoined the original Warrington line at Carterhouse Junction. One track of the old route was still in situ on 4th June 1997 as no. 31554 passed with the Runcorn Folly Lane – Arpley trip of salt hoppers ultimately bound for Dalry. The LNW box of 1896 originally had 30 levers and backed onto the St Helens Canal. It was switched out in 2001 and officially closed from 3rd December 2006. Industry continued for a further half mile beyond Carter House and was served by British Alkali signal box. The first on the site served from 1879-96 and its replacement thence until 12th June 1955. Both were situated on the down side adjacent to a swing bridge across the canal. (D.Birmingham)

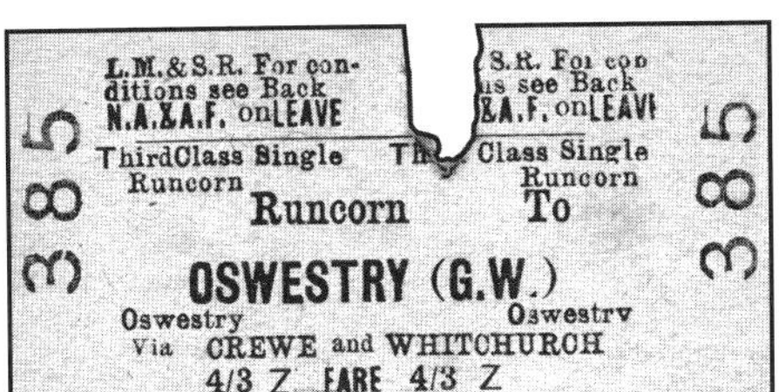

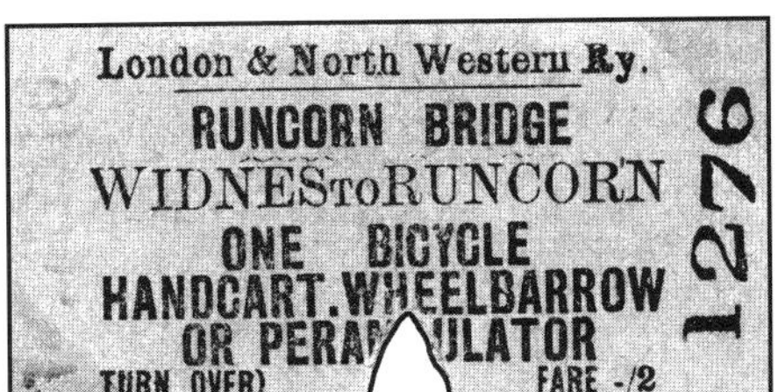

Cuerdley

This short-lived station (November 1855 to 5th January 1858) was two miles from Runcorn Gap. The lane from Cuerdley Cross was later subsumed by the power station.

WEST OF FIDLERS FERRY & PENKETH

Fiddlers Ferry Power Station

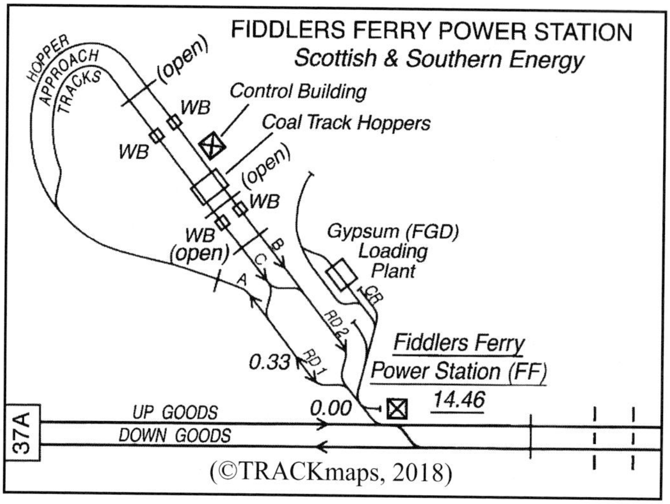

(©TRACKmaps, 2018)

XXI. The site of this 2,000-megawatt coal-fired power station, 2 miles east of Widnes, was chosen in the early 1960s because it was a major greenfield site close to abundant water (for cooling) and adjacent to a railway line that no longer had the inconvenience of a passenger service. It was constructed under the management of the Central Electricity Generating Board and was one of a new generation of large power stations that operated on the Merry Go Round principle, whereby each trainload of coal was taken around a loop line during which it discharged its wagons into a huge underground bunker. The empty train departed whence it came without the locomotive having had to uncouple or even completely stop. Construction began in 1964 but it was another seven years before full production started.

Meanwhile the railway facilities were installed, including an east facing junction and signal box (called Fidlers Ferry Power Station with a single 'd') which was operational from 30th July 1967. The grand plan was to ship the coal from South Yorkshire, using goods only routes. This worked well until BR closed the Woodhead route across the Pennines in 1981. Not long afterwards came the miners' strike of 1984-85, which was followed by widespread pit closures, not least in South Yorks. Alternative sources of supply were necessary, and coal was increasingly imported. This was usually hauled from Liverpool Docks via Edge Hill (reverse), Ditton Junction, Latchford Sidings (beyond Warrington, reverse), and back to the power station.

After privatisation of electricity generation in 1990 the power station had various owners, latterly Scottish & Southern Energy. As a consequence of international climate accords it closed on 31st March 2020. During the time it was in use, the UK's primary energy sources had moved from almost complete reliance on fossil fuels to renewables.

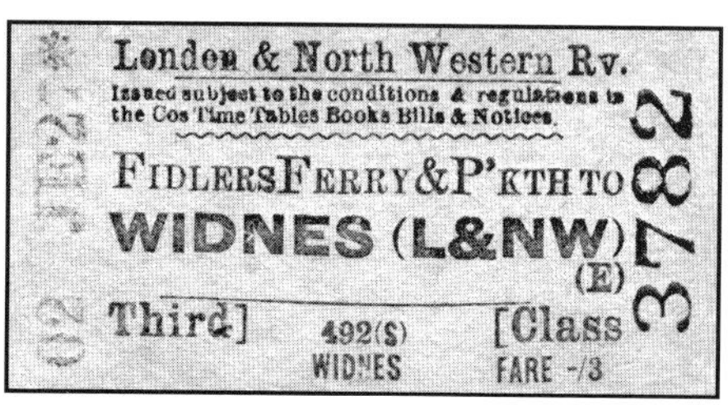

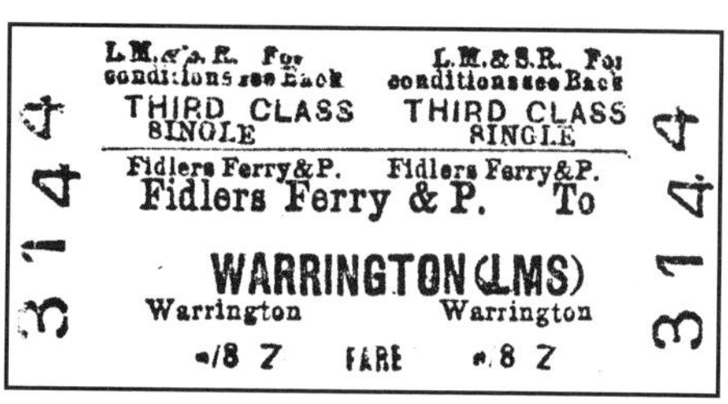

99. On 9th May 1991 a loaded coal train from Bickershaw colliery approaches the power station behind nos 20159 and 20195. Note the flat roofed signal box at left; the junction was just beyond. The shunt signal is off and the scene is reflected in the St Helens Canal. The power station had eight cooling towers, each 375ft tall, and a 600ft chimney. (D.Birmingham)

100. On 22nd October 1997 we are taken inside the power station and see no. 56031 running at slow speed through the discharge hopper with the once familiar HAA wagons that have travelled from Silverdale colliery. (D.Birmingham)

FIDLERS FERRY & PENKETH

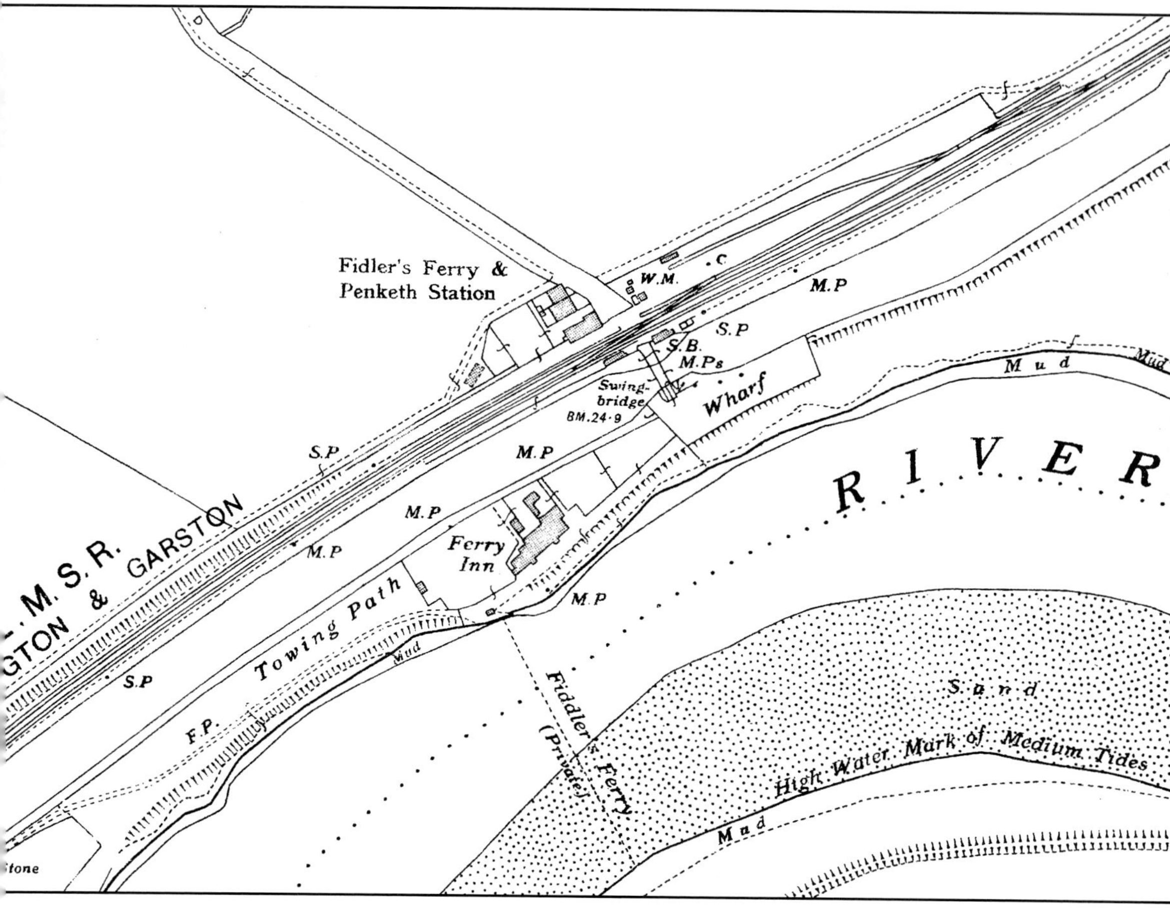

XXII. The station was 3½ miles from Widnes and opened with the line as Fiddlers Ferry. It was renamed Fiddlers Ferry & Penketh in April 1881, and Fidlers Ferry & Penketh in either 1920 or 1921. Penketh was ½ mile to the north. The station closed to passengers from 2nd January 1950 and to goods from 2nd December 1963. Opinion is divided between those who believe the station name was apostrophised, ie Fidler's, at the time of closure and those who believe it followed local practice and was not. We have adopted the latter which is the form carried by the 1967 signal box.

The Sankey Brook Navigation Canal had reached here, where it entered the River Mersey, around 1765 when it was extended from Sankey Bridges. It was further extended to Runcorn Gap on 24th July 1833 and the Runcorn Gap to Warrington railway later followed its course as far as Sankey Bridges. This map is dated 1939.

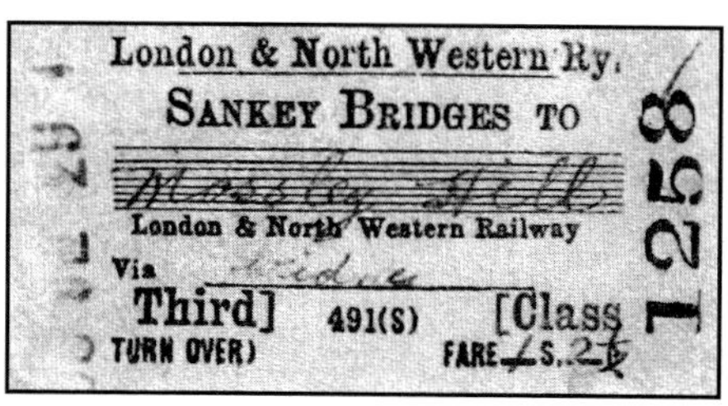

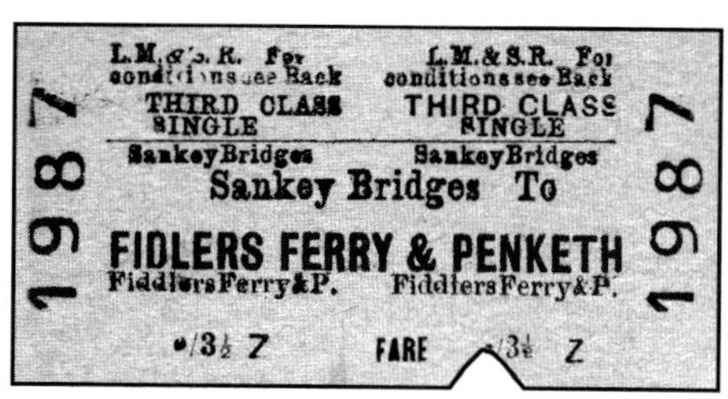

101. This is a westward view from 1901. The station buildings to the right of the line comprise a pair of railwaymen's cottages fronting Station Road, the single storey booking office/waiting room on the up platform, and the Saxby & Farmer signal box of 1880. The photographer is standing on the goods siding. On the down platform is a modest shelter. A train has just departed towards Widnes. (*Disused-stations.org.uk*)

102. On 4th January 1964 an 8F 2-8-0 heads towards Widnes with what appear to be wooden-bodied coal trucks. The cottages and station building can be seen, along with an LNW signal box which replaced the original on the opposite side of the line in 1904. The box closed on 1st May 1965 and was demolished along with the station soon afterwards.
(H.Arnold/*Disused-stations.org.uk*)

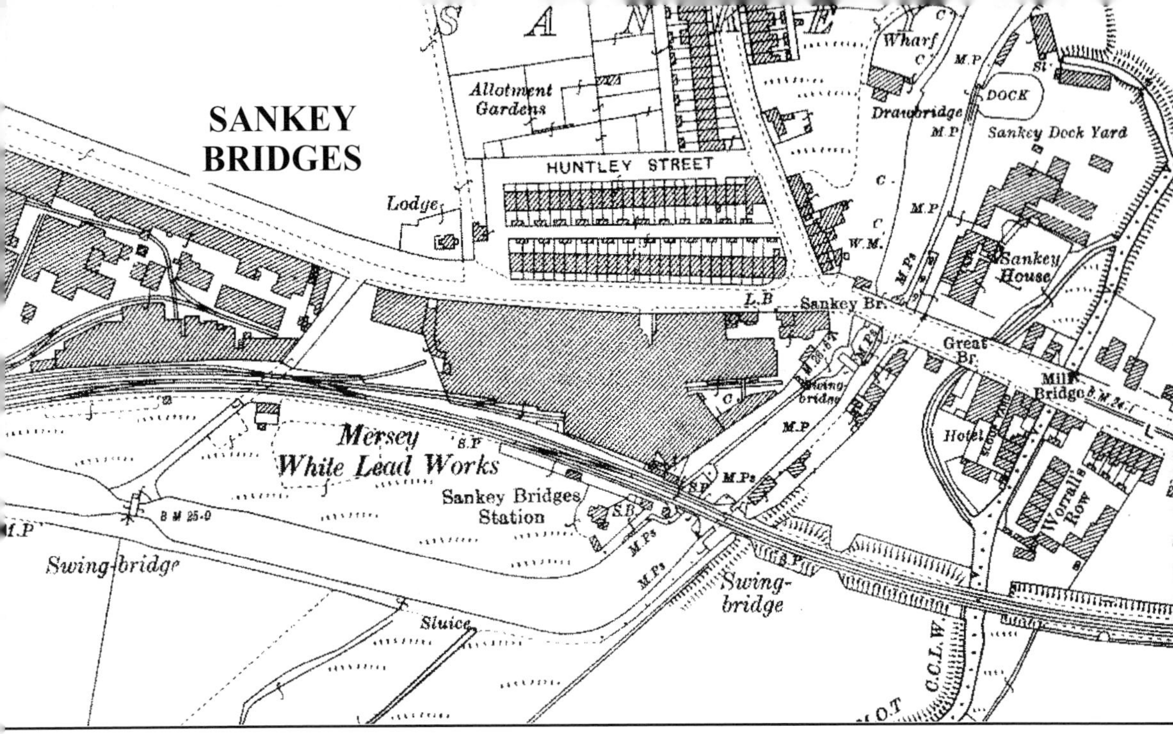

XXIII. This was 4¾ miles from Widnes and 1½ miles from Warrington Bridge. Warrington Corporation Tramways located its western terminus, also called Sankey Bridges, adjacent to Mill Bridge on Liverpool Road in 1902, and by the time the system closed in 1935 there were frequent buses. The station was an early closure from 26th September 1949, having also been closed between 1st January 1917 and 30th June 1919. There was no public goods facility, but the Mersey White Lead Works, Sankey Wire Mills, and the Polar refrigeration works all had private sidings. The map is dated 1925.

103. We have been unable to find a pre-closure picture of the station. This image dates from 17th September 1961 and looks west. In the foreground the line crossed the St Helens Canal on a swing bridge that was by now out of use. The canal originally joined Sankey Brook here for ¾ mile before it flowed into the Mersey. The signal box closed in March 1964. The factories marked the transition of the line's route across the quiet Mersey marshes to industrial Warrington. (P.Norton/*Disused-stations.org.uk*)

WEST OF WARRINGTON BANK QUAY LOW LEVEL

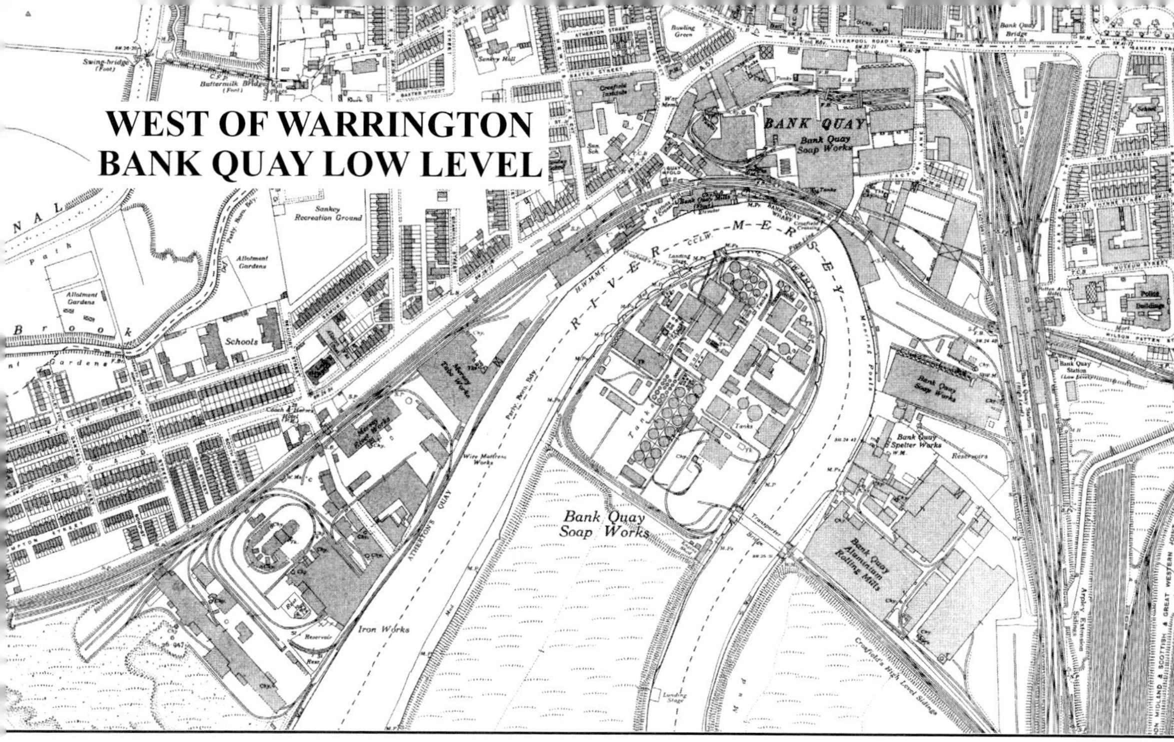

XXIV. From Sankey Bridges to Warrington Bank Quay was around one mile, much of which became lined with factories producing iron, wire, flour and soap. Most had rail connections. When the line from Runcorn Gap opened on 1st February 1853 it was obliged to end temporarily at Whitecross, around ⅝ mile from Sankey Bridges, whilst the LNW main line at Bank Quay was raised to accommodate it. It eventually opened to Arpley, east of the map, on 1st May 1854 where it made an end-on connection with the Warrington & Stockport Railway. The map is dated 1937.

104. On 13th October 1986 no. 47381 hauls empty HAA wagons from Fidlers Ferry past Monks Siding box ½ mile beyond Sankey Bridges. The track at left formerly accessed the Atherton Quay iron works of Monks Hall & Co. The site of the works was subsequently redeveloped for housing. The signal box dates from 1875. At right is the Coach & Horses public house which is marked on the map. (J.Whitehouse)

105. Littons Mill Crossing was 25 chains east of Monks Siding. Named for the nearby flour mill this 18-lever installation was the second box at the site and dated from 1890. Here it is seen on 13th October 1986 as no. 25109 passes with empty mineral wagons. It closed on 16th July 2012. (J.Whitehouse)

106. Only 10 chains separated Littons Mill and Crosfields Crossing boxes. The latter dated from 1907 and had an 18-lever frame of which ultimately only four were in use following the closure of its associated sidings. It also closed on 16th July 2012 but continued in use as a relay room. Here it is seen in the early 1990s as no. 60045 *Josephine Butler* passes with MGR coal empties from Fidlers Ferry and threads its way through the Crosfields site on its approach to Bank Quay. (B.Morrison)

WARRINGTON BANK QUAY LOW LEVEL

After the SHCR was taken over, the LNW decided to relocate its Warrington station to the crossing of the south to north and west to east lines at Bank Quay. The combined station opened on 16th November 1868 and provided low level platforms on the former SHCR.

The last passenger services on the Low Level ran on 8th September 1962 except for one train a week, the Sunday Liverpool–York mail. This called at Bank Quay shortly before midnight and last ran on 13th June 1965.

107. On 28th April 1948 LMS class 3P 2-6-2T no. 207 has drawn up next to the water crane whilst working the 6.05pm Liverpool Lime Street – Manchester Oxford Road local. We see the single storey platform buildings with their generous canopies beyond the rear of the train, and the main line station crossing our route in the background. (W.A.Camwell/ Stephenson Loco Soc.)

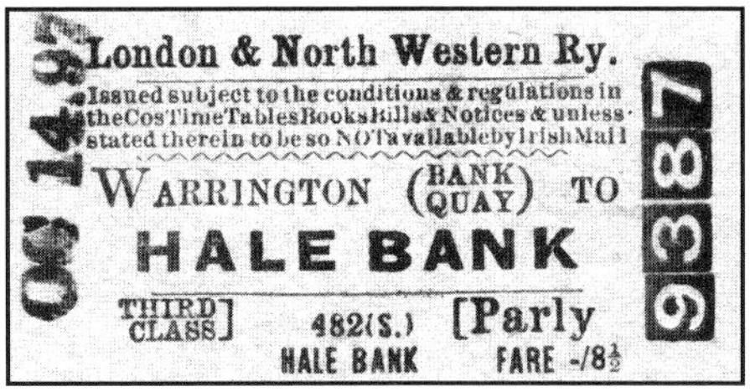

London & North Western Ry.
Issued subject to the conditions & regulations in the Cos Time Tables Books Bills & Notices & unless stated therein to be so NOT available by Irish Mail
WARRINGTON (BANK QUAY) TO
HALE BANK
THIRD CLASS 482(S.) [Parly
HALE BANK FARE -/8½
9387

The line onward to Arpley and Broadheath will be covered in a future volume. For views of the main station, see *Chester to Warrington (via Frodsham)* and *Crewe to Wigan (including the Over & Wharton branch)*.

108. In mid-1961 a Manchester Oxford Road – Ditton Junction push-pull service with 2MT 2-6-2T no. 41288 on the rear stands at the down platform. Opposite is the up platform, and at right is the up bay platform and beyond that a former horse dock. Behind them we see the main station entrance building. Electric lighting has replaced gas but Crosfields soap works continue to dominate the background. (L.Fifoot coll./*Disused-stations.org.uk*)

4. Runcorn Gap – Farnworth & Bold

RUNCORN GAP (WIDNES DOCK)

We return to map XX (near picture 92) and turn our attention to the line running from Widnes Dock to the top, the LMS St Helens line. The Widnes side of the Runcorn Gap was chosen for the establishment of a dock to be served by the SHRG, which received Royal Assent on 29th May 1830. The line formally opened on 21st February 1833 and the dock on 26th July 1833. The St. Helens Canal effectively separated the dock area from the township. The railway crossed the canal by a swing bridge to enter the dock area, and the passenger platform was on the town side of the bridge.

When the Garston branch opened on 1st July 1852, Runcorn Gap station was relocated ¼ mile westward on the new route (see picture 93). On 1st September 1864 it was renamed Widnes and on 1st March 1870 it was relocated a second time (see pictures 94-96). No pictures are known of either of the early stations. When the Warrington line opened in 1853 it was joined to the Garston line to permit through running. This link crossed the original north to south line of 1833 on the flat. The arrangement was called Widnes Dock Junction and it soon became very busy.

109. On 11th April 1959 we see one reason why the flat crossing was subject to congestion – it was used by local factories as well as by main line trains. Here Albright & Wilson's (AW) Peckett 0-4-0ST, works no. 1852 of 1933, is apparently propelling ICI wagons from the Warrington direction, possibly en route from ICI's Muspratt Works to AW's factory at Ann Street. This involved passing westward over the flat crossing, beneath the leftmost tanker, and then drawing back along the Garston Curve. At right we see the curve linking Widnes Dock with the line to Warrington. In this highly industrialised image we can see at least three more wagons on two different sidings. The long footbridge is prominent (see picture 97). (J.A.Peden/IRS)

110. This picture from 1960 shows the southern end of the SHRG line; the first passenger station was close to the loading bay canopy on the factory to the right of the train leaving the dock hauled by a WD 8F 2-8-0; the rear end of the train is crossing the canal swing bridge. The lines to the left are running towards Warrington, and the track to the right, on which a 350hp diesel shunter is waiting to proceed, leads to the West Bank Estate. In the foreground we can just see part of the flat crossing. In the background note the Runcorn Bridges (see picture 66). Widnes Dock closed in 1931 and was filled in. Its sidings continued to be used for wagon storage until 4th November 1968. (E.Bellass/R.Mercer coll./8D Association)

111. On 5th August 1967 the LCGB ran the Warrington & Widnes Brake Van railtour which covered most of the former LNW lines in the Widnes area. Hauled by BR 4MT 2-6-0 no. 76077 it was posed at the flat crossing standing on the Garston – Warrington line. The signal box is Widnes No. 4 (Dock Junction) which closed from 10th March 1969 along with the remaining lines at this location. Note the signals visible above its roof that were on the Deviation line. (J.M.Tolson/Catalyst Museum)

ANN STREET

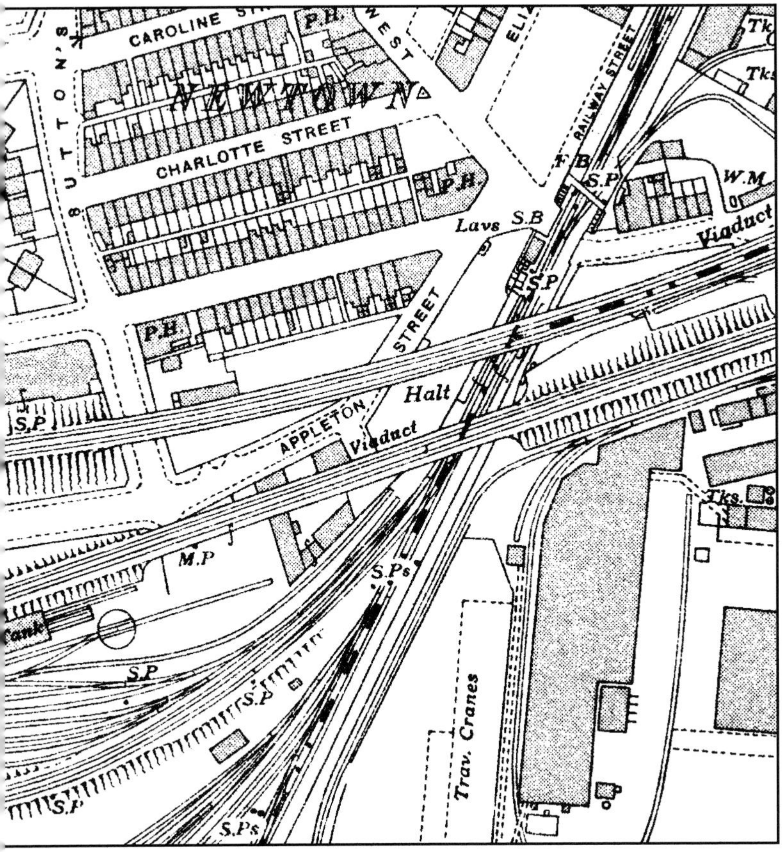

XXV. Ann Street opened on 1st October 1911 as a railmotor halt and closed with the cessation of the passenger service on 18th June 1951. We have been unable to find a photograph of the halt, which was almost certainly of light-weight timber construction. The short platforms appear to have been staggered because of limited space. The up (northbound) platform was between the bridges carrying the Deviation line and the LNE/LMS line (marked on the map as 'Halt') and the down platform was between the latter and Ann Street level crossing, which was adjacent to the signal box. The map is dated 1937.

112. This fine study of Widnes No. 2 signal box was taken on 16th June 1939. The photographer is standing on or adjacent to the north end of the down platform. On the left we see houses on Appleton Street. The double signal guards Ann Street level crossing, just off the right of the picture, and we can see the gate wheel through the right-hand window of the box. The box itself was built in 1895 when it replaced the original installation of 1869; it was a standard LNW design and had 35 levers. It lasted until 13th January 1974 when the crossing was automated with lifting barriers.
(R.J.Buckley/
Initial Photographics)

113. Taken in 1966 from a footbridge that was added to the already busy scene in the 1950s we see an 8F 2-8-0 running south. The bridge carrying the LNE/LMS line, opened in 1877 and demolished soon after the line closed in 1964, crossed our route above the loco, and its abutments can be seen on either side. The space between the right-hand line and the low wall visible above the signal arm was the site of Ann Street's up platform. The loco has just reached the junction with the route to the Deviation line, which itself crosses the bridge ahead. The second junction just visible beyond the bridge is between the original line to Runcorn Gap heading straight on, and the Garston Curve. Widnes No. 3 signal box, known as Loco Junction, was located here between 1874 and 1931. (R.Mercer/*Disused-stations.org.uk*)

114. On 31st July 1970 we look north from the site of the up platform as Type 3 diesel no. 6916 runs south with four car transporter wagons bound for Ford Halewood. At left we see Widnes No. 2 signal box with Ann Street level crossing beyond. Behind the loco is the truncated viaduct of the LNE/LMS line. (R.Mercer/8D Association)

NORTH OF ANN STREET

Referring once again to map XX, ¼ mile beyond Ann Street the line was bridged by Warrington Road, the A562. Widnes No. 1 signal box stood immediately to the south of the bridge on the up side having replaced an earlier box in 1893. To its south were numerous private goods sidings particularly on the down side east of the route. The siding that led from Widnes No. 1 to Tanhouse Lane ('Sta.' next to the Golden Bowl Hotel) was upgraded to main line status from 16th March 1961 to provide direct access from the north to the USAC sulphuric acid factory. The latter was located at Moss Bank and started production in 1955. One of the by-products of the process was cement, and when the factory closed in 1973 distribution continued using cement railed in from Hope, Derbyshire. Following the closure of the LNE/LMS line from 6th December 1964 all traffic for Tanhouse Lane was worked via Widnes No. 1. From 1st November 1981 the SHRG closed north of Widnes No. 1, and Tanhouse Lane – Widnes No. 1 – Widnes South followed from 18th April 1982. A new connection was made from the Deviation line to serve Tanhouse Lane, which was used until rail traffic ceased in 2000. The A557 trunk road linking the M62 with Runcorn Silver Jubilee Bridge was built over the formation of the SHRG between Widnes and Farnworth in 1993/94.

115. On 3rd March 1980 no. 08887 is hauling empty wagons to Hutchinson Street Goods past Widnes No. 1 box which can be seen above the sixth wagon. The train has come along the line at right from the Blue Circle cement sidings at Tanhouse Lane. (B.Roberts/8D Association)

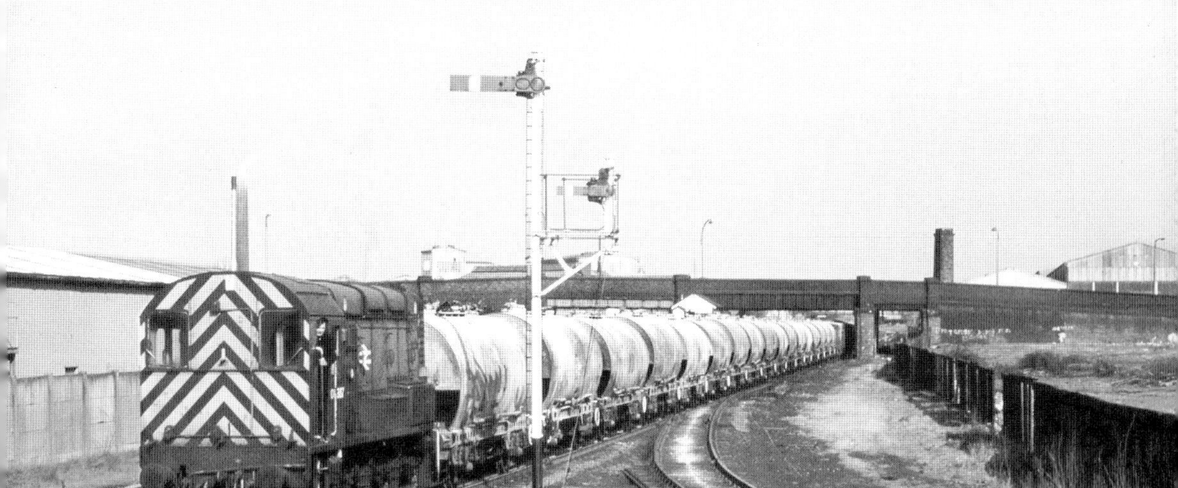

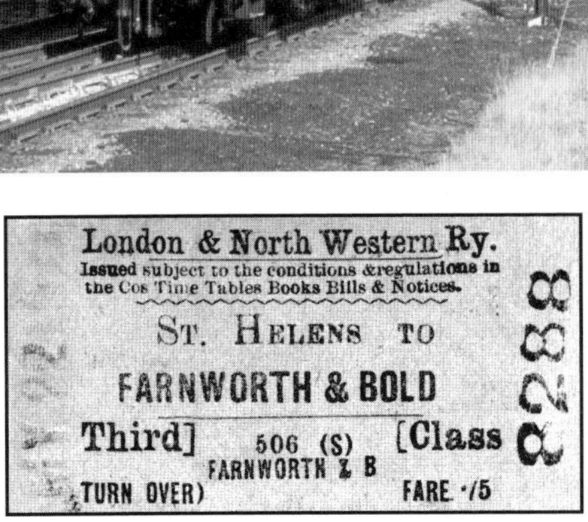

APPLETON

XXVI. The SHRG initially had a 1:29 rope worked incline between Appleton, which was one mile north of Runcorn Gap, and Farnworth. This was eliminated in 1850 by realignment, and in 1852 a passenger timetable was published for the first time. This included a station at Appleton. Goods were not handled here although there were private sidings. The map is dated 1937.

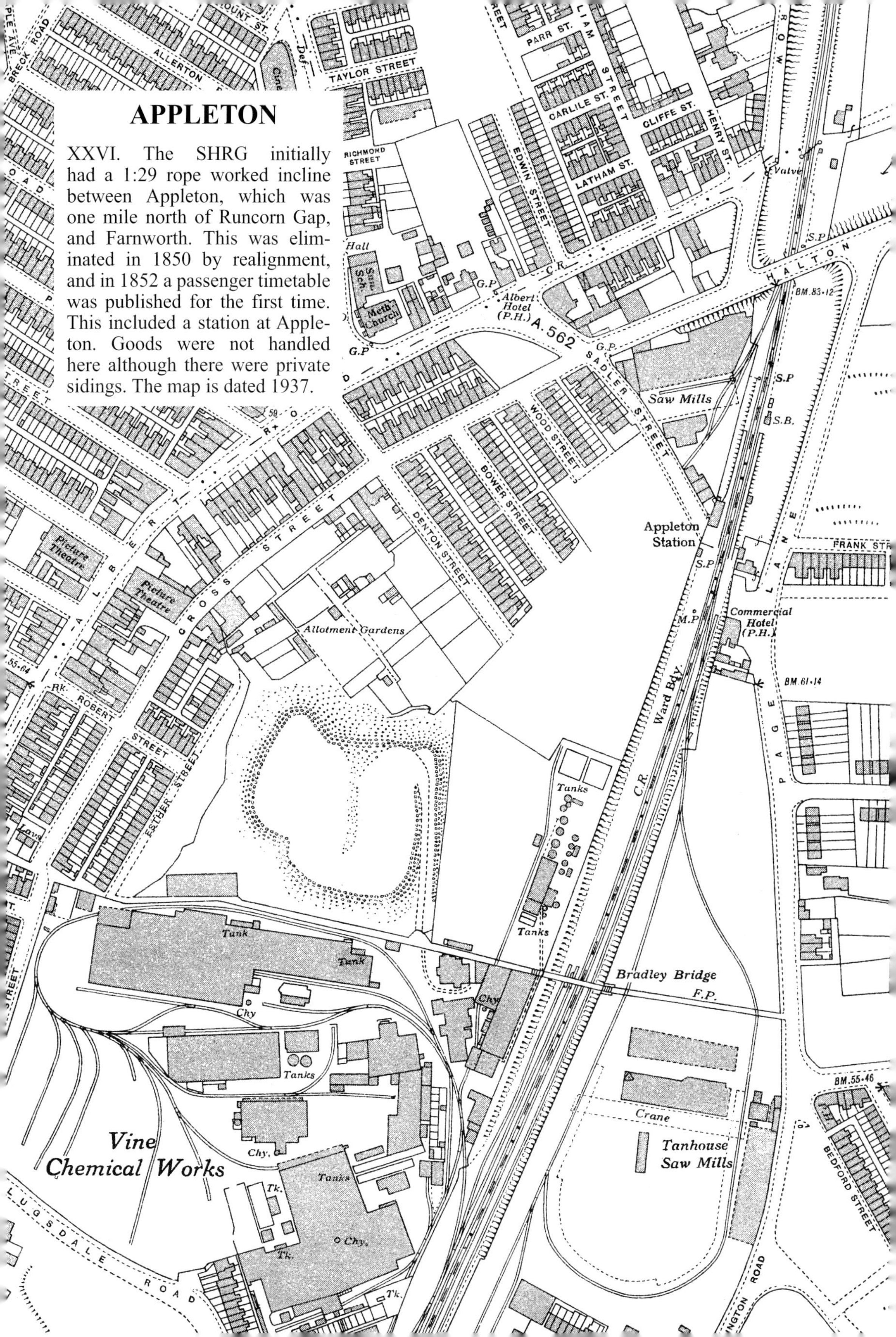

116. This northward view is thought to date from the early 1880s. The modest main station building is on the up side. The first signal box, installed in 1879, can be seen in the distance guarding the level crossing with Halton View Road. The box was abolished in 1904, probably when the crossing was replaced by a bridge, and an LNW box was built close to the station. (I.Deakin coll/*Disused-stations.org.uk*)

117. There were no great changes between the opening of the new signal box and the closure of the station in 1951. Even then the signal box lasted until the end of 1966 and the main station building stood until the line closed. The track was singled between Widnes No. 1 signal box and Farnworth on 4th November 1973. This was the view from the Halton View Road bridge on 10th January 1962 when 'Jubilee' 4-6-0 no. 45581 *Bihar and Orissa*, an unusual visitor from Leeds Farnley Junction shed, stormed past on empty coal hoppers. The business on the right was a saw mill, rail connected until c1958. (J.M.Tolson/Catalyst Museum)

FARNWORTH & BOLD

XXVII. Farnworth station was actually at Barrow's Green, one mile north of Appleton, and opened at the same time. It was renamed Farnworth & Bold from 2nd January 1890 to avoid confusion with the CLC's Farnworth station less than a mile away. Passenger closure was from 18th June 1951 and goods from 1st June 1964. The line closed from 1st November 1981 following the end of traffic to Turners Everite factory. The map is dated 1938.

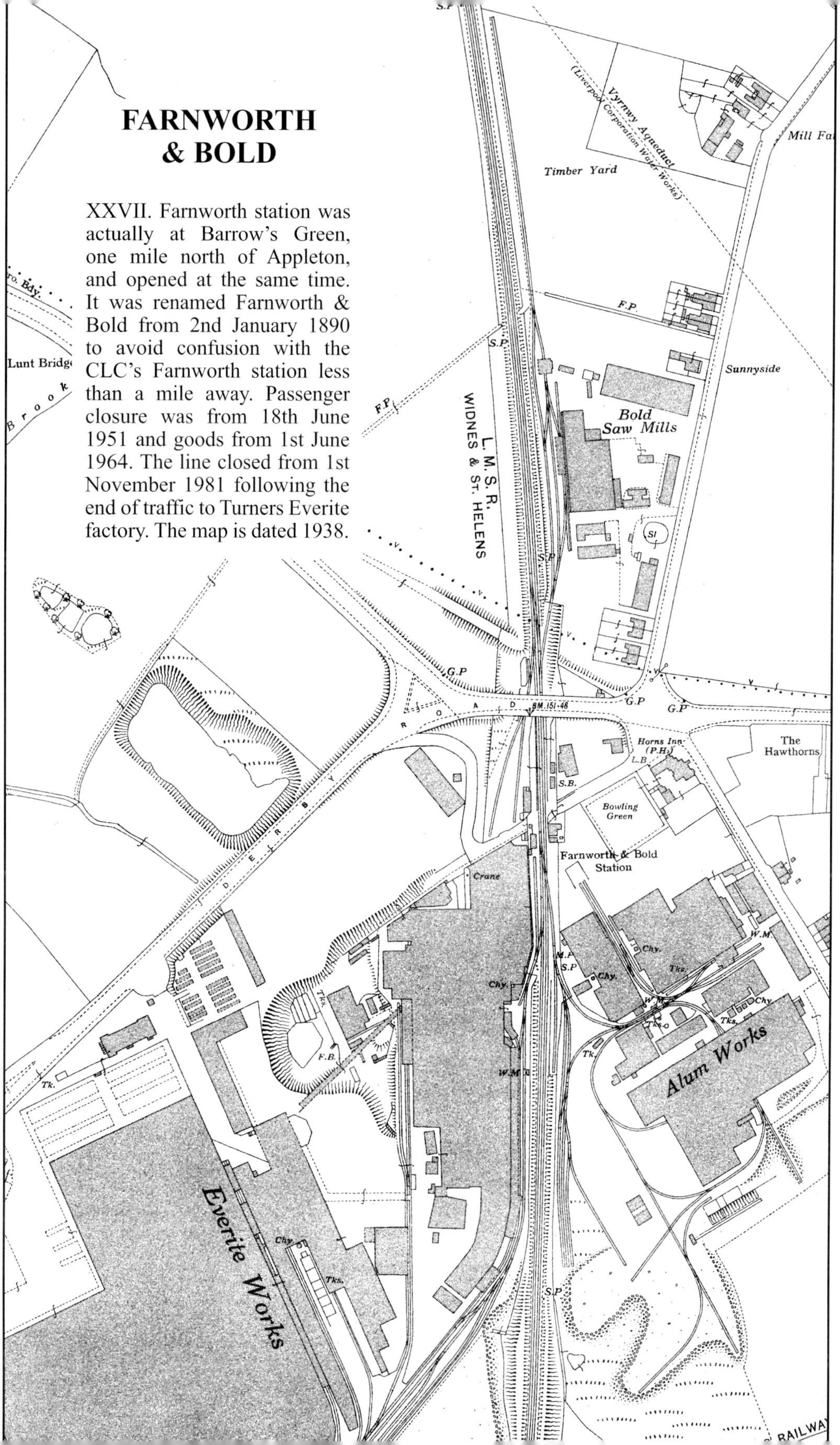

118. We start with a southward view from the bridge carrying the Liverpool – Warrington road, later the A5080, of a St Helens – Ditton Junction service in 1904. From left to right we see the signal box, modest main station building on the opposite platform, and goods facilities behind it. Open countryside can be seen to the south-west, but that would change. (J.Alsop coll./*Disused-stations.org.uk*)

➔ 119. Now we look north in 1939 at a down Ditton Dodger in push-pull mode. The bridge replaced a level crossing in the 1870s, and the LNW signal box replaced the original Saxby & Farmer box in 1920. (SSPL/*Disused-stations.org.uk*)

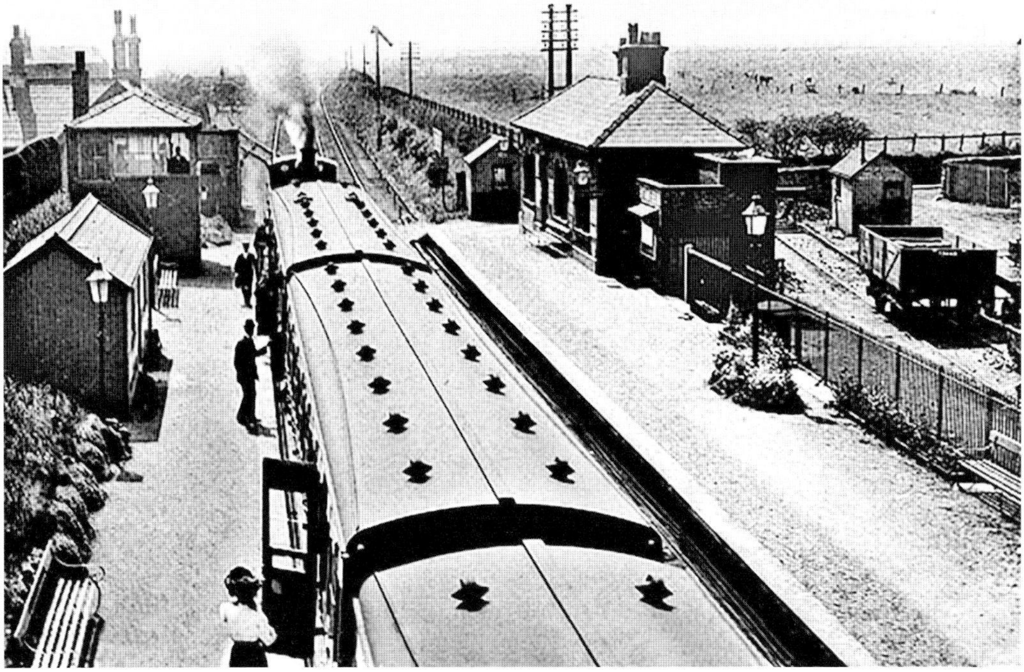

➔ 120. This 1958 view from the road bridge shows an annual works outing from Widnes to Blackpool for the employees of Thomas Boulton & Sons, hauled by an unidentified Jubilee 4-6-0. The station presents a tidy appearance despite having closed seven years previously; it was quite possibly re-opened on occasion for excursions such as this. The fields south of the station have disappeared beneath factories. The one on the right was Turners Asbestos, and south-west of that was the related Everite Works. These generated rail traffic between 1916 and 1981. Note the sign partially obscured by the signal box which reads 'Goods trains to stop to pin down brakes', a reminder there was a 1:70 gradient down to Appleton. The signal box closed on 4th November 1973. The station building was not demolished until c1992. (G.Howarth/Catalyst Museum)

Beyond Farnworth & Bold the line continued to Clock Face, Sutton Oak and St Helens Shaw Street, and will be covered in a future volume.

A
Abergavenny to Merthyr C 91 8
Abertillery & Ebbw Vale Lines D 84 5
Aberystwyth to Carmarthen E 90 1
Allhallows - Branch Line to A 62 8
Alnmouth to Berwick G 50 0
Alton - Branch Lines to A 11 6
Ambergate to Buxton G 28 9
Ambergate to Mansfield G 39 5
Andover to Southampton A 82 6
Ascot - Branch Lines around A 64 2
Ashburton - Branch Line to B 95 4
Ashford - Steam to Eurostar B 67 1
Ashford to Dover A 48 2
Austrian Narrow Gauge D 04 3
Avonmouth - BL around D 42 5
Aylesbury to Rugby D 91 3

B
Baker Street to Uxbridge D 90 6
Bala to Llandudno E 87 1
Banbury to Birmingham D 27 2
Banbury to Cheltenham E 63 5
Bangor to Holyhead F 01 7
Bangor to Portmadoc E 72 7
Barking to Southend C 80 2
Barmouth to Pwllheli E 53 6
Barry - Branch Lines around D 50 0
Bartlow - Branch Lines to F 27 7
Basingstoke to Salisbury A 89 4
Bath Green Park to Bristol C 36 9
Bath to Evercreech Junction A 60 4
Beamish 40 years on rails E94 9
Bedford to Wellingborough D 31 9
Berwick to Drem F 64 2
Berwick to St. Boswells F 75 8
B'ham to Tamworth & Nuneaton F 63 5
Birkenhead to West Kirby F 61 1
Birmingham to Wolverhampton E253
Blackburn to Hellifield F 95 6
Bletchley to Cambridge D 94 4
Bletchley to Rugby E 07 9
Bodmin - Branch Lines around B 83 1
Bolton to Preston G 61 6
Boston to Lincoln F 80 2
Bournemouth to Evercreech Jn A 46 8
Bradshaw's History F18 5
Bradshaw's Rail Times 1850 F 13 0
Branch Lines series - see town names
Brecon to Neath D 43 2
Brecon to Newport D 16 6
Brecon to Newtown E 06 2
Brighton to Eastbourne A 16 1
Brighton to Worthing A 03 1
Bristol to Taunton D 03 6
Bromley South to Rochester B 23 7
Bromsgrove to Birmingham D 87 6
Bromsgrove to Gloucester D 73 9
Broxbourne to Cambridge F16 1
Brunel - A railtour D 74 6
Bude - Branch Line to B 29 9
Burnham to Evercreech Jn B 68 0
Buxton to Stockport G 32 6

C
Cambridge to Ely D 55 5
Canterbury - BLs around B 58 9
Cardiff to Dowlais (Cae Harris) E 47 5
Cardiff to Pontypridd E 95 6
Cardiff to Swansea E 42 0
Carlisle to Beattock G 69 2
Carlisle to Hawick E 85 7
Carmarthen to Fishguard E 66 6
Caterham & Tattenham Corner B251
Central & Southern Spain NG E 91 8
Chard and Yeovil - BLs a C 30 7
Charing Cross to Orpington A 96 3
Cheddar - Branch Line to B 90 9
Cheltenham to Andover C 43 7
Cheltenham to Redditch D 81 4
Chesterfield to Lincoln G 21 0
Chester to Birkenhead F 21 5
Chester to Manchester F 51 2
Chester to Rhyl E 93 2
Chester to Warrington F 40 6
Chichester to Portsmouth A 14 7
Clacton and Walton - BLs to F 04 8
Clapham Jn to Beckenham Jn B 36 7
Cleobury Mortimer - BLs a E 18 5
Clevedon & Portishead - BLs to D180
Consett to South Shields E 57 4
Cornwall Narrow Gauge D 56 2
Corris and Vale of Rheidol E 65 9
Coventry to Leicester G 00 5
Craven Arms to Llandeilo E 35 2
Craven Arms to Wellington E 33 8
Crawley to Littlehampton A 34 5
Crewe to Manchester F 57 4
Crewe to Wigan G 12 8
Cromer - Branch Lines around C 26 0
Cromford and High Peak G 35 7
Croydon to East Grinstead B 48 0
Crystal Palace & Catford Loop B 87 1
Cyprus Narrow Gauge E 13 0

D
Darjeeling Revisited F 09 3
Darlington Leamside Newcastle E 28 4
Darlington to Newcastle D 98 2
Dartford to Sittingbourne B 34 3
Denbigh - Branch Lines around F 32 1
Derby to Chesterfield G 11 1
Derby to Nottingham G 45 6
Derby to Stoke-on-Trent F 93 2
Derwent Valley - BL to the D 06 7
Devon Narrow Gauge E 09 3
Didcot to Banbury D 02 9
Didcot to Swindon C 84 0
Didcot to Winchester C 13 0
Diss to Norwich G 22 7
Dorset & Somerset NG D 76 0
Douglas - Laxey - Ramsey E 75 8
Douglas to Peel C 88 8
Douglas to Port Erin C 55 0
Douglas to Ramsey D 39 5
Dover to Ramsgate A 78 9
Drem to Edinburgh G 06 7
Dublin Northwards in 1950s E 31 4
Dunstable - Branch Lines to E 27 7

E
Ealing to Slough C 42 0
Eastbourne to Hastings A 27 7
East Croydon to Three Bridges A 53 6
Eastern Spain Narrow Gauge E 56 7
East Grinstead - BLs to A 07 9
East Kent Light Railway A 61 1
East London - Branch Lines of C 44 4
East London Line B 80 0
East of Norwich - Branch Lines E 69 7
Effingham Junction - BLs a A 74 1
Ely to Norwich C 90 1
Enfield Town & Palace Gates D 32 6
Epsom to Horsham A 30 7
Eritrean Narrow Gauge E 38 3
Euston to Harrow & Wealdstone C 89 5
Exeter to Barnstaple B 15 2
Exeter to Newton Abbot C 49 9
Exeter to Tavistock B 69 5
Exmouth - Branch Lines to B 00 8

F
Fairford - Branch Line to A 52 9
Falmouth, Helston & St. Ives C 74 1
Fareham to Salisbury A 67 3
Faversham to Dover B 05 3
Felixstowe & Aldeburgh - BL to D 20 3
Fenchurch Street to Barking C 20 8
Festiniog - 50 yrs of enterprise C 83 3
Festiniog 1946-55 E 01 7
Festiniog in the Fifties B 68 8
Festiniog in the Sixties B 91 6
Ffestiniog in Colour 1955-82 F 25 3
Finsbury Park to Alexandra Pal C 02 8
French Metre Gauge Survivors F 88 8
Frome to Bristol B 77 0

G
Gainsborough to Sheffield G 17 3
Galashiels to Edinburgh F 52 9
Gloucester to Bristol D 35 7
Gloucester to Cardiff D 66 1
Gosport - Branch Lines around A 36 9
Greece Narrow Gauge D 72 2
Guildford to Redhill A 63 5

H
Hampshire Narrow Gauge D 36 4
Harrow to Watford D 14 2
Harwich & Hadleigh - BLs to F 02 4
Harz Revisited F 62 8
Hastings to Ashford A 37 6
Hawick to Galashiels F 36 9
Hawkhurst - Branch Line to A 66 6
Hayling - Branch Line to A 12 3
Hay-on-Wye - BL around D 92 0
Haywards Heath to Seaford A 28 4
Hemel Hempstead - BLs to D 88 3
Henley, Windsor & Marlow - BLa C77 2
Hereford to Newport D 54 8
Hertford & Hatfield - BLs a E 58 1
Hertford Loop E 71 0
Hexham to Carlisle D 75 3
Hexham to Hawick F 08 6
Hitchin to Peterborough D 07 4
Horsham - Branch Lines to A 02 4
Hull, Hornsea and Withernsea G 27 2
Hull to Scarborough G 60 9
Huntingdon - Branch Line to A 93 2

I
Ilford to Shenfield C 97 0
Ilfracombe - Branch Line to B 21 3
Ilkeston to Chesterfield G 26 5
Ipswich to Diss F 81 9
Ipswich to Saxmundham C 41 3
Isle of Man Railway Journey F 94 9
Isle of Wight Lines - 50 yrs C 12 3
Italy Narrow Gauge F 17 8

K
Kent Narrow Gauge C 45 1
Kettering to Nottingham F 82-6
Kidderminster to Shrewsbury E 10 9
Kingsbridge - Branch Line to C 98 7
Kings Cross to Potters Bar E 62 8
King's Lynn to Hunstanton F 58 1
Kingston & Hounslow Loops A 83 3
Kingswear - Branch Line to C 17 8

L
Lambourn - Branch Line to C 70 3
Launceston & Princetown - BLs C 19 2
Leeds to Selby G 47 0
Leek - Branch Line From G 01 2
Leicester to Burton F 85 7
Leicester to Nottingham G 15 9
Lewisham to Dartford A 92 5
Lincoln to Cleethorpes F 56 7
Lincoln to Doncaster G 03 6
Lines around Newmarket G 54 8
Lines around Stamford F 98 7
Lines around Wimbledon B 75 6
Lines North of Stoke G 29 6
Liverpool to Runcorn G 72 2
Liverpool Street to Chingford D 01 2
Liverpool Street to Ilford C 34 5
Llandeilo to Swansea E 46 8
London Bridge to Addiscombe B 20 6
London Bridge to East Croydon A 58 1
Longmoor - Branch Lines to A 41 3
Looe - Branch Line to C 22 2
Loughborough to Ilkeston G 24 1
Loughborough to Nottingham F 68 0
Lowestoft - BLs around E 40 6
Ludlow to Hereford E 14 7
Lydney - Branch Lines around E 26 0
Lyme Regis - Branch Line to A 45 1
Lynton - Branch Line to B 04 6

M
Machynlleth to Barmouth E 54 3
Maesteg and Tondu Lines F 06 2
Majorca & Corsica Narrow Gauge F 41 3
Manchester to Bacup G 46 3
Mansfield to Doncaster G 23 4
March - Branch Lines around B 09 1
Market Drayton - BLs around F 67 3
Market Harborough to Newark F 86 4
Marylebone to Rickmansworth D 49 4
Melton Constable to Yarmouth Bch E031
Midhurst - Branch Lines of E 78 9
Midhurst - Branch Lines to F 00 0
Minehead - Branch Line to A 80 2
Monmouth - Branch Lines to E 20 8
Monmouthshire Eastern Valleys D 71 5
Moretonhampstead - BL to C 27 7
Moreton-in-Marsh to Worcester D 26 5
Morpeth to Bellingham F 87 1
Mountain Ash to Neath D 80 7

N
Newark to Doncaster F 78 9
Newbury to Westbury C 66 6
Newcastle to Alnmouth G 36 4
Newcastle to Hexham D 69 2
Newmarket to Haughley & Laxfield G 71 5
New Mills to Sheffield G 44 9
Newport (IOW) - Branch Lines to A 26 0
Newquay - Branch Lines to C 71 0
Newton Abbot to Plymouth C 60 4
Newtown to Aberystwyth E 41 3
Northampton to Peterborough F 92 5
North East German NG D 44 9
Northern Alpine Narrow Gauge F 37 6
Northern Spain Narrow Gauge E 83 3
North London Line B 94 7
North of Birmingham F 55 0
North of Grimsby - Branch Lines G 09 8
North Woolwich - BLs around C 65 9
Nottingham to Boston F 70 3
Nottingham to Kirkby Bentinck G 38 8
Nottingham to Lincoln F 43 7
Nottingham to Mansfield G 52 4
Nuneaton to Loughborough G 08 1

O
Ongar - Branch Line to E 05 5
Orpington to Tonbridge B 03 9
Oswestry - Branch Lines around E 60 4
Oswestry to Whitchurch E 81 9
Oxford to Bletchley D 57 9
Oxford to Moreton-in-Marsh D 15 9

P
Paddington to Ealing C 37 6
Paddington to Princes Risborough C819
Padstow - Branch Line to B 54 1
Peebles Loop G 19 7
Pembroke and Cardigan - BLs to F 29 1
Peterborough to Kings Lynn E 32 1
Peterborough to Lincoln F 89 5
Peterborough to Newark F 72 7
Plymouth - BLs around B 98 5
Plymouth to St. Austell C 63 5
Pontypool to Mountain Ash D 65 4
Pontypridd to Merthyr F 14 7
Pontypridd to Port Talbot E 86 4
Porthmadog 1954-94 - BLa B 31 2
Portmadoc 1923-46 - BLa B 13 8
Portsmouth to Southampton A 31 4
Portugal Narrow Gauge E 67 3
Potters Bar to Cambridge D 70 8
Preston to Blackpool G 16 6
Preston to Lancaster G 74 6
Princes Risborough - BL to D 05 0
Princes Risborough to Banbury C 85 7

R
Railways to Victory C 16 1
Reading to Basingstoke B 27 5
Reading to Didcot C 79 6
Reading to Guildford A 47 5
Redhill to Ashford A 73 4
Return to Blaenau 1970-82 C 64 2
Rhyl to Bangor F 15 4
Rhymney & New Tredegar Lines E 48 2
Rickmansworth to Aylesbury D 61 6
Romania & Bulgaria NG E 23 9
Ross-on-Wye - BLs around E 30 7
Ruabon to Barmouth E 84 0
Rugby to Birmingham E 37 6
Rugby to Loughborough F 12 3
Rugby to Stafford F 07 9
Rugeley to Stoke-on-Trent F 90 1
Ryde to Ventnor A 19 2

S
Salisbury to Westbury B 39 8
Salisbury to Yeovil B 06 0
Sardinia and Sicily Narrow Gauge F 50 5
Saxmundham to Yarmouth C 69 7
Saxony & Baltic Germany Revisited F 71 0
Saxony Narrow Gauge D 47 0
Scunthorpe to Doncaster G 34 0
Seaton & Sidmouth - BLs to A 95 6
Selsey - Branch Line to A 04 8
Sheerness - Branch Line to B 16 2
Sheffield towards Manchester G 18 0
Shenfield to Ipswich E 96 3
Shrewsbury - Branch Line to A 86 4
Shrewsbury to Chester E 70 3
Shrewsbury to Crewe F 48 2
Shrewsbury to Ludlow E 21 5
Shrewsbury to Newtown E 29 1
Sirhowy Valley Line E 12 3
Sittingbourne to Ramsgate A 90 1
Skegness & Mablethorpe - BL to F 84 0
Slough to Newbury C 56 7
South African Two-foot gauge E 51 2
Southampton to Bournemouth A 42 0
Southend & Southminster BLs E 76 5
Southern Alpine Narrow Gauge F 22 2
South London Line B 46 6
South Lynn to Norwich City F 03 1
Southwold - Branch Line to A 15 4
Spalding - Branch Lines around E 52 9
Spalding to Grimsby F 65 9 6
Stafford to Chester F 34 5
Stafford to Wellington F 59 8
St Albans to Bedford D 08 1
St. Austell to Penzance C 67 3
St. Boswell to Berwick F 44 4
Stourbridge to Wolverhampton E 16 1
St. Pancras to Barking D 68 5
St. Pancras to Folkestone E 88 8
St. Pancras to St. Albans C 78 9
Stratford to Cheshunt F 53 6
Stratford-u-Avon to Birmingham D 77 7
Stratford-u-Avon to Cheltenham C 25 3
Sudbury - Branch Lines to F 19 2
Surrey Narrow Gauge C 87 1
Sussex Narrow Gauge C 68 0
Swaffham - Branch Lines around F 97 0
Swanage to 1999 - BL to A 33 8
Swanley to Ashford B 45 9
Swansea - Branch Lines around F 38 3
Swansea to Carmarthen E 59 8
Swindon to Bristol C 96 3
Swindon to Gloucester D 46 3
Swindon to Newport D 30 2
Swiss Narrow Gauge C 94 9

T
Talyllyn 60 E 98 7
Tamworth to Derby F 76 5
Taunton to Barnstaple B 60 2
Taunton to Exeter C 82 6
Taunton to Minehead F 39 0
Tavistock to Plymouth B 88 6
Tenterden - Branch Line to A 21 5
Three Bridges to Brighton A 35 2
Tilbury Loop C 86 4
Tiverton - BLs around C 62 8
Tivetshall to Beccles D 41 8
Tonbridge to Hastings A 44 4
Torrington - Branch Lines to B 37 4
Tourist Railways of France G 04 3
Towcester - BLs around E 39 0
Tunbridge Wells BLs A 32 1

U
Upwell - Branch Line to B 64 0
Uttoxeter to Macclesfield G 05 0
Uttoxetor to Buxton G 33 3

V
Victoria to Bromley South A 98 7
Victoria to East Croydon A 40 6
Vivarais Revisited E 08 6

W
Walsall Routes F 45 1
Wantage - Branch Line to D 25 8
Wareham to Swanage 50 yrs D 09 8
Waterloo to Windsor A 54 3
Waterloo to Woking A 38 3
Watford to Leighton Buzzard D 45 6
Wellingborough to Leicester F 73 4
Welshpool to Llanfair E 49 9
Wenford Bridge to Fowey C 09 3
Wennington to Morecambe G 58 6
Westbury to Bath B 55 8
Westbury to Taunton C 76 5
West Cornwall Mineral Rlys D 48 7
West Croydon to Epsom B 08 4
West German Narrow Gauge D 93 7
West London - BLs of C 50 5
West London Line B 84 8
West Wiltshire - BLs of D 12 8
Weymouth - BLs A 65 9
Willesden Jn to Richmond B 71 8
Wimbledon to Beckenham C 58 1
Wimbledon to Epsom B 62 6
Wimborne - BLs around A 97 0
Wirksworth - Branch Lines to G 10 4
Wisbech - BLs around C 01 7
Witham & Kelvedon - BLs a E 82 6
Woking to Alton A 59 8
Woking to Portsmouth A 25 3
Woking to Southampton A 55 0
Wolverhampton to Shrewsbury E 44 4
Wolverhampton to Stafford F 79 6
Worcester to Birmingham D 97 5
Worcester to Hereford D 38 8
Worthing to Chichester A 06 2
Wrexham to New Brighton F 47 5
Wroxham - BLs around F 31 4

Y
Yeovil - 50 yrs change C 38 3
Yeovil to Dorchester A 76 5
Yeovil to Exeter A 91 8
York to Scarborough F 23 9